RESEARCH STUDIES IN EARLY CHILDHOOD EDUCATION

RESEARCH STUDIES IN EARLY CHILDHOOD EDUCATION

Edited by Cathy Nutbrown

Trentham Books

Stoke on Trent, UK and Sterling, USA

Trentham Books Limited

Westview House	22883 Quicksilver Drive
734 London Road	Sterling
Oakhill	VA 20166-2012
Stoke on Trent	USA
Staffordshire	
England ST4 5NP	

© 2002 Cathy Nutbrown

First published 2002

Reprinted 2003

British Library Cataloguing-in-Publication Data
A catalogue record for this book is available from the British Library

1 85856 270 8

Designed and typeset by Trentham Print Design Ltd., Chester and printed in Great Britain by Cromwell Press Ltd., Wiltshire.

Grateful thanks to Peter Clough and Sage Publications for permission to use the diagram on page 161.

Contents

About the contributors

Editor
Dr. Cathy Nutbrown directs the MA in Early Childhood Education at the University of Sheffield. She has an international reputation for her research and is author of numerous publications in the field of early childhood education. Publications include: *Threads of Thinking* (PCP, 1999), *Experiencing Reggio Emilia* (Nutbrown and Abbott OUP, 2001), *Respectful Educators – Capable Learners* (PCP, 1997) and *A Students' Guide to Methodology: Justifying Enquiry* (Clough and Nutbrown Sage, 2002)

Contributors
Sue Allingham is Foundation Stage and Infant Co-ordinator in a London primary school.

Tracey Berry teaches children with autistic spectrum disorders. She is mathematics co-ordinator for her school and a Leading Maths Teacher for Hartlepool LEA.

Julie Bravery is Senior Curriculum Advisor for the Foundation Stage and Key Stage one, supporting schools and the Early Years and Childcare Partnership in Essex.

Di Chilvers was a Local Authority Advisory Teacher and is now a senior lecturer in Early Childhood Studies.

Debbie Critchley is a teacher trainer, and until recently taught young Emirati women to become primary school teachers of English in the UAE, in conjunction with Melbourne University. Debbie has worked in Jordan and Spain and is now at the British Council in Cairo.

Polly Dyer is the nursery teacher and Foundation Stage leader in a Primary school in Brighton.

Gill Farmer spent some years working with young children and their families in the voluntary sector and now teaches students in Further and Higher Education.

Vicky Grant is currently senior nursery nurse in a nursery class of 40 children in a small co-ed independent school in Edinburgh.

Ramona Khan lives and works in Trinidad and Tobago where she trains preschool educators working within the SERVOL network.

Anne Kirkpatrick was a Key Stage 1 teacher (with responsibility for literacy and co-ordinating key stage 1) until 2000 and is now studying for a PhD at the University of Sheffield.

Christine Parker has taught in England and in Pakistan and is head teacher of a nursery school in the south of England.

Nicky Walters is an enthusiastic early years teacher who has recently taught in British Forces schools in Cyprus. She is now Early Years Advisory Teacher in Plymouth.

Sue Webster was an outreach worker in a multi-service Early Excellence Centre in the south of England. She is currently Curriculum Advisor in Oxfordshire.

Preface

Early Childhood Education is central to the government's stated aim of providing an integrated and inclusive system of lifelong learning from cradle to grave. This book makes a distinctive contribution to the critical debate relating to that policy agenda. The research it reports should be widely read by practitioners, policy-makers and researchers with an interest in, and commitment to, ensuring all-through educational provision for all our children.

There are three important aspects of the research accounts provided in the following pages. First, they focus on what is acknowledged to be a highly significant grey area between policy specification and practical application. As the following accounts make abundantly clear, it is misleading to conceptualise practice simply as the unproblematic implementation of policy: as if the former could be 'read off' from the latter. Policy formation is a highly complex process within which practice speaks back to policy and, in so doing, shapes the ends and purposes of both. The following accounts have the potential to contribute greatly to our understanding of how policy travels and of how, in its travels, policy is subject to competing pressures and demands.

Second, the accounts provide some fine instances of practitioner research. We can trace in these accounts the indirect influence of three overlapping traditions which have had a profound effect on educational research and teacher education over the last forty years: the tradition of 'teacher-as-researcher' developed by Lawrence Stenhouse; of 'classroom action research' as supported by John Elliott and others; and of the 'reflective practitioner' as advanced by Donald Schon. The book refuses to proselytise on behalf of these traditions and should, perhaps, be read against their grain. It carries these traditions forward and provides its own implicit critique of the way in which those traditions have sometimes unwittingly allowed themselves to become inward-looking and remote from the key policy issues of the day.

Third, the book challenges its readers to acknowledge the importance of inter-agency perspectives and ways of working. The authors are drawn from a range of institutional contexts and backgrounds and are all centrally concerned with ensuring that Early Childhood Education engages with families and communities. By implication it re-defines professionalism in terms of inter-professional collaboration and community-oriented change. It relates directly to the current emphasis on joined-up policy and integrated provision and on the need for practitioners and policy makers alike to work at strengthening the links between institutions and across sectors.

The contributions to this volume are further evidence, if such were needed, that the study of Early Childhood Education is at the forefront of the current policy debate on the development of educational systems that are coherent, differentiated and inclusive in respect of individual need.

Professor Jon Nixon
Head of School of Education
University of Sheffield

Introduction

In 1999 a group of early childhood educators came together to discuss research and practice in an international context. They came together because they wanted to understand the wider world of early childhood education and because they wanted to make a difference in their own professional contexts.

The contributors to this volume describe work which has been developed in their own early childhood settings and contexts in England, Scotland, Cyprus, Trinidad and Tobago and the United Arab Emirates.

The chapters cover various territories of enquiry in early childhood education but what pervades the collection is a sense of concern with issues of citizenship and with social justice. It is against those contexts that current Early Childhood Education policies are examined and critiqued. In sharing something of their small-scale research studies, the authors open up opportunities for discussion of several policy developments and offer original perspectives on various curricular concerns.

What is refreshing is the fact that curriculum discussion is not confined to the policy-restricted discussions of literacy and numeracy, but offers dynamic discussions on, for example, teaching for well-being, inclusion, gender and equality. Policy discussions portray practitioners' experiences of how it is, day in – day out – and how it might be if policy were *interpreted* by informed practitioners rather than simply *implemented*. The studies reported here demonstrate a realisation that the policy-aware educator is positioned to make a difference.

The contributors in this volume do not always provide 'end-points' to their enquiries, because many of the experiences represented here are part of the continuing stories which will each have their own distinct responses to policy and to change.

I should like to thank all the contributors who willingly and enthusiastically agreed to share their work, and also Andrew and Bethany Nutbrown for their never-ending support. My deep appreciation goes also to many colleagues in the School of Education at The University of Sheffield: Wilfred Carr, Peter Clough, Judi Duffield, Peter Hannon, Kath Hirst, Jackie Marsh, Jon Nixon, Lorraine Roe and Rachel Watson. They have supported the completion of this collection in different ways, but the contribution of every one of them has been essential. I am indeed blessed to work with such generous colleagues.

Cathy Nutbrown

1

Early Childhood Education in contexts of change

Cathy Nutbrown

How comes change? We read of its coming in the books of history – 'change was in the air', 'that was the decisive year', 'then came the breakthrough', but when we live through history it is quite different: change takes place on the ground not in the air, each year seems only too much like the next, and as for the breakthrough – we wait for it in vain. Yet, looking back over a period, somehow change has come. (Schiller, 1979)

The inevitability of change

Early Childhood Education is different now. In England and Wales, policies of the 1990s have changed, forever, state-funded systems, services and practices. Through its policy of funding alternative, voluntary and independent preschool education (such as Montessori nurseries, preschool playgroups and fee-paying independent schools) the UK government has also influenced the curriculum of non-state provision.

The radical and far-reaching policy influences in Early Childhood Education in England and Wales of the 1990s has inevitably impacted upon the specific and generic practices of early childhood educators. State prescribed curriculum for children below the statutory school starting age was heralded in 1996 with what was called *Desirable Outcomes of Nursery Education on Entry to Compulsory Schooling*, later amended and concretised in 2000 with government recommendations for curriculum for children aged 3–5+years (QCA, 2000). State required assessment was introduced in

1998 (SCAA, 1997) under the National Framework for Baseline Assessment. For the first time in England and Wales four year olds (children below the age of compulsory schooling) were required to be assessed. Discomfort of practitioners and dissatisfaction of policy makers reigned until 2002 when necessary changes were made to adjust the point (and focus) of nationally reported assessment.

Many practitioners had by then won back their confidence in making professional judgements about the learning needs and achievements of young children and so were influencing the nature of the assessments as well as the purposes to which the results were put. The two policies, of curriculum (QCA, 2000) and Baseline Assessment (SCAA, 1997), – unpopular with the majority of Early Childhood Educators – resulted in an assessment-led preschool curriculum which threatened the broadly inclusive nature of early childhood education provision. Other policy initiatives followed; the National Literacy Strategy (DfEE 98), the National Numeracy Strategy QCA, 1999), the Codes of Practice for Special Educational Needs (DfEE, 1994, DfES, 2001). Each had their own particular impact on Early Childhood Education, but the collective effect of these policies was a narrowing of curriculum and reforming of provision such that it became less and less appropriate for many young children and militated especially against the inclusion of children with Special Educational Needs.

The flurry of hurried policy responses to perceived difficulties within the education system of the 1990s plunged Early Childhood Education into changes in practice, at a pace and depth never before experienced. In the fifteen years from 1988 to 2002, early childhood educators have

- implemented the National Curriculum and subsequent revisions

- faced newly introduced, rigorous and stressful inspection processes

- worked with the implementation of the Children Act 1989

- worked to interpret expected 'outcomes' of nursery education

- worked with new codes of practice for the identification of children with Special Educational Needs

- implemented changes in relation to national assessment of children on entry to school

- worked with diminishing resources and increasing expectations

- worked with diminishing support and limited opportunities for professional development

- grappled with issues affecting the teaching of four year olds in school

- worked within a developing network of diversity of provision and Early Years Child Care Partnerships

- implemented aspects of the National Literacy Strategy

- implemented aspects of the National Numeracy Strategy

- implemented new curriculum developed from Government guidance

- transformed the Foundation Stage from policy to practice

- adapted to revisions in Assessment in the context of the Foundation Stage

This represents no less that fifteen different policy initiatives in as many years, an average of one major policy change each year. Within this context of continual change there has been great concern that an over-emphasis of 'academic' achievement (particularly in literacy and numeracy) was resulting in neglect of children's emotional well being (Roberts, 1995). The pace and extent of policy development left no element of state-funded Early Childhood Education provision untouched. Little wonder that there was a recruitment problem in some parts of the country.

The undeniable legacy of history

... there have been great men and women whose vision and action have inspired a generation: Robert Owen, Friedrich Froebel, in our own time Margaret McMillan and others. But they pass away, and their ideas pass away with them unless these ideas are fashioned into new forms which reflect new circum-

stances and stand the test of new practices in the contemporary scene. The
pioneers take such ideas and refashion and temper them in their daily work in
school. Patiently, day after day, week after week and year after year they make
the pathway from the past through the present towards the future. (Christian
Schiller, 1951 pxvii)

With those policy changes came a denial of the history of Early
Childhood Education – a seemingly deliberate ignorance of the
achievements and lessons of the past. Policy documents throughout
the 1990s seemed to ignore the history of Early Childhood Education and its legacy of philosophy, pedagogy and purpose. This denial
was most apparent (and most commented upon) in the almost total
absence of the word 'play' from official documents which seemed to
be imposing a new language of early education (Nutbrown, 1998).
Early childhood educators had to learn to speak this language in
order to maintain their status as actors on the education stage, but
backstage the real drama was taking place. After consistent and un-
relenting lobbying and clear demonstrations to policy makers of the
importance of maintaining some of the historical legacy of influential pioneers was acknowledged, the use of play in Early Childhood Education regained its official recognition (QCA, 2000). However, the denial of the history of Early Childhood Education ran
deeper than this: policy documents made no reference to previous
research of recent history or practice in the UK or overseas and contained no recognition of the published work of pioneers such as
Froebel, Isaacs, McMillan and others who had so influenced Early
Childhood Education provision in the UK and Europe. It caused
some modern writers to draw attention to the dangers of ignoring
historical influences:

> *Taking account of the past and using it means a continuity with progression,*
> *rather than stop-start ways of working with different factions rising and falling*
> (Bruce et al., 1995 pxiii)

Suddenly it seemed that Early Childhood Education in the UK had
no roots and no history. In its place there was stand-alone late 20th
Century policy. Many young teachers had no introduction to Isaacs,
Piaget or Vygotsky, to academic rationale for learning through play,
to child development theories, to the importance of observation-
based assessment. This was because the requirements for the initial
training of teachers laid down the curriculum and study require-

ments to the extend that only a handful of Higher Education establishments were able to maintain their high quality training courses for early childhood teachers. The new generation of early childhood teachers had become *implementers* rather than *interpreters* of policy, with no means of fully understanding or properly articulating the policy contexts in which they were working.

Early Childhood Education had changed, in just over a decade, from a grounded and evolving response to meeting the learning needs of young children, into a hastily constructed response to modern policy. Another viewpoint – without the benefit of history – would be that Early Childhood Education in England and Wales had suddenly received government recognition – government ministers talked about 'the under fives' with increasing frequency and policies of health, education and community featured discussion of provision for the youngest children. Viewed from this modern perspective, there was political recognition, but viewed through the lens of history such recognition was only partial and missed the 'big picture'. Without history it is impossible fully to understand the present.

> An analysis of the past can help us to understand what is happening now and to anticipate what may happen in the future in schools. Just as every teacher's behaviour in school is influenced by his or her own personal and professional experiences, so every school is influenced by a range of local, political, economic and personal changes and in turn every LEA is influenced by wider political and social changes. An awareness of these imperatives can make things that are happening in schools that appear incomprehensible suddenly become clear. (Anning, 1997, p1)

But in this context of incessant change, something was stirring in the consciousness of early childhood educators and the realisation of the importance of what is past as a platform for the future drew on research to challenge the wrongs in new policies. But to where did they turn?

Into the future: citizenship and social justice
Albert Einstein said:

> It is a fact nothing short of a miracle that the modern methods of instruction have not yet entirely strangled the holy curiosity of inquiry; for this delicate little plant, aside from stimulation, stands mainly in need of freedom; without this it goes to wrack and ruin without fail.

Throughout the legacies of history, international conflicts, and the undaunted work of yesterday's and today's pioneers, those with a commitment to providing the best they can for children in their earliest years have debated the ingredients of curriculum and the responsibilities of educators. If we have learned anything from the history of Early Childhood Education – wherever the education of the young takes place – Steiner schools, Montessori nurseries, Preschool Playgroups, Reggio Emilia preschools, state governed nurseries and schools, reception classes, independent schools – surely we have learned that successful education of young children depends on the development of a *healthy culture of relationships*. Those relationships depend upon learning with and from others, in our own learning communities and beyond – into wider local, national and international contexts. Such learning depends on an understanding of the nature of citizenship and a commitment to strive for social justice.

The dissemination of information and the potential for human contact and communication (albeit sometimes virtual) means that it is possible for early childhood educators world wide to exchange understandings. There is no excuse for ignorance of the work of others, and every opportunity to act in the interests of young children as global citizens. With greater sharing of research and practices we can recover freedom: freedom to act together, freedom to learn, freedom to question, freedom to understand, and the freedom to be different.

There is a rich variety of approaches to teaching and learning in Early Childhood Education in the UK and around the world. What is important is not so much the identification of the best single approach, but the reaching of shared understandings of various approaches and thus shared principles on which our work is based. And with that we may develop a shared understanding of what drives us and a shared language with which to articulate our work.

How comes change...?
We can look back and say nothing has changed, for example parents, educators and governments still worry over the safety of the youngest citizens. The need to protect children is not new, but the threats to their well being have changed over the past century. Robert Owen's first school for infants in New Lanark provided a haven for

the young children of factory workers in the early 1800s, catering for their physical and intellectual needs and ensuring some space to play (Owen 1824). In the 1920s the MacMillan sisters promoted good health as well as learning in their 'Open Air' nurseries with fresh air, hot food and cleanliness being the priorities for children from the slum areas of British cities, many of whom suffered the effects of poverty, including rickets and malnutrition (Aldrich and Gordon, 1989).

Security, emotional security, can be born of the predictability of rhythm and repetition but children also need protection from physical harm. In one weekend newspaper in early January 2001 I found four articles, each given at least half a page of broadsheet space, which demonstrated just how threatening our world can be: depleted uranium in Sarajevo where children played in a contaminated bomb crater; the abuse, torture and murder of an eight-year-old girl in a London flat; controversy in the UK over the measles, mumps and rubella (MMR) vaccine alleged to cause or contribute to autism in some children; the kidnapping of a six-year-old child in the Philippines. Such articles appear on the television news and in our newspapers with such regularity that we sometimes become numbed to their horror. The threats to safety can be rolled off the tongue with alarming familiarity: BSE, GM foods, mobile phones, immunisation, traffic pollution, pollution of the seas and rivers... the list could go on.

Arguably, it was Susan Isaacs who moved on thinking about the education of the young to include their immense capacity to imitate and imagine in their play. Isaacs left an enduring legacy of understanding children's play in the detailed observations of children who attended her Malting House School 1924-1927 (Isaacs, 1954). Provision for and the threats to children's play were debated throughout the 20th Century. Niko Tinbergen (1976) wrote an article called *The importance of being playful* in which he identified the different experiences for children whose parents once played outdoors unsupervised, making mud pies, free to explore and children who could no longer enjoy such things. He warned that nurseries were forced to create the 'muddy field' in a small tray of clay, and puddles and rivers were replaced by the 'water trough'. So what happens when those children become parents? How do parents who have never experienced the importance of being playful understand and create the opportunities for their own children to know what playing – really playing – is? These questions raise important issues for all early childhood educators. How might children be free to play while at the same time being protected? How might this be achieved and how can history help us here?

> *'I'd like to go to a school where there was a beautiful garden, and trees, and woods, and flowers, and in the middle of the garden there would be a cool pool, a big pool where the dolphins swim...'*

Six-year-old Martha had her own clear idea of what a perfect school should be like. It should be a place where the beauty of nature was right at the heart of everything that happened. *In the middle* would be calm and grace and beauty. Had Martha met the HMI Christian Schiller, they might have had an interesting conversation about what schools should be like, and what children should do in them. In 1946 Schiller set out his characteristics of a 'good' school as follows:

- *the school conceives of primary education, not as a preparation for something to follow, but as a fulfilment of a stage of development*

- *the school seeks to achieve this fulfilment, not by securing certain standards of attainment, but by providing in abundance such experience and activities as will enable all the children to develop to the full at each phase of growth*

- *the children are expressing their powers in language, in movement, in music, in painting, and in making things – that is to say, as artists*

- *the children are developing their powers in language, in observation, in counting, and in the use of the body – that is to say, as workmen*

- *the children are learning to live together to the best advantage*

- *the children's need for movement and for rest determine the arrangement of experience and activities, and how much the children get out of an experience or activity determines the amount of time given to it.*

(Schiller, 1946 in Griffiths-Blake (ed) 1979 p3)

I have chosen six of Schillers' many characteristics of a 'good' school. But it is clear that for this member of Her Majesty's Inspectorate the values which underpinned education were the needs and capabilities of children *as perceived by an adult.* Thus was constructed a view of childhood as a time of active engagement, of exploration and a time too where adults must provide them protection. Looking at the past offers us the opportunity to create environments for learning where children achieve their potential as artists, as workers and, crucially, as actively contributing citizens in a learning community.

References

Abbott, L. and Moylett, H. (1999) *Working with the Under Threes: supporting children's needs* Buckingham: Open University Press

Aldrich, R. and Gordon, P. (1989) *Dictionary of British Educationists* London: Woburn Press

Bruce,T., Findlay, A., Read, J. and Scarborough, M. (1995) *Recurring Themes in Education* London: Paul Chapman Publishing

DfEE (1994) *Code of Practice on the Identification and Assessment of Special Educational Needs* London: Stationery Office

DfEE (1998) *The National Literacy Strategy* London: DfEE

DfEE (1999) *Code of Practice on the Identification and Assessment of Special Educational Needs* (Revised) London: DfEE

DfES (2001) *Code of Practice on the Identification and Assessment of Special Educational Needs* (Revised) London: DfES

DfEE (1999) *The National Numeracy Strategy* London DfEE

Isaacs, S, (1954) *The Educational Value of the Nursery School* London. British Association of Early Childhood Education

Nutbrown, C. (1999) *Threads of Thinking: Young children learning and the role of early education* London: Paul Chapman Publishing

Nutbrown, C. (ed) (1997) *Respectful Educators – Capable Learners: children's rights and early education* London: Paul Chapman Publishing

Owen, R (1824) An outline of the system at New Lanark (Glasgow 1824) pp32-33 – Select Committee on Education of the Lower Orders of the Metropolis (London 1816: 1968 edition)

QCA (2000) *Curriculum Guidance for the Foundation Stage* London: Qualifications and Curriculum Authority

Roberts, R. (1995) *Developing Children's Self-esteem and Early Childhood Education* London: Hodder and Stoughton

SCAA (1997) *National Framework for Baseline Assessment: criteria and procedures for the accreditation of Baseline Assessment Schemes* London: School Curriculum and Assessment Authority

Schiller, C (1951) How comes change? In Schiller, C (1979) *Christian Schiller in his own words.* Edited by C. Griffiths-Blake London: National Association for Primary Education

Schiller, C (1979) *Christian Schiller in his own words.* Edited by C. Griffiths-Blake London: National Association for Primary Education

Tinbergen, N. (1976) *The Importance of Being Playful* London: British Association of Early Childhood Education

Woodhead, M. (1996) *In Search of the Rainbow* Netherlands: The Van Leer Foundation

Part I

TEACHING, LEARNING AND ASSESSMENT IN THE FOUNDATION STAGE

2

Policy influences on learning and teaching in the reception year

Sue Allingham

It is the skill of the educator to be aware of the pieces of the jigsaw that the child already has in place and whether or not they have been fitted together correctly. (Fisher, J., 1996. p7)

Overview

This chapter examines recent national policy initiatives to influence teaching and learning in reception classes in England and Wales.

As new policy initiatives are introduced and implemented they should be evaluated by those working with them to ascertain their value and appropriateness. A central question in this study was the extent to which good Early Years practice might be influenced and changed by the introduction of a 'Foundation Stage' (QCA, 2000).

Defining and identifying quality

Fisher (1996) defines good early years practice thus:

> *It is the skill of the educator to be aware of the pieces of the jigsaw that the child already has in place and whether or not they have been fitted together correctly. If they have not, then supporting the child to review the construction of their cognitive jigsaw is as delicate and difficult an operation as persuading the child to select an alternative piece of wooden puzzle. The 'teacher' – whether an adult or another child- needs to be informative without being imposing. Imposition simply leads to the learner becoming confused and disaffected. Confusion arises because the links between the pieces have been made by the teacher and not the learner. Disaffection occurs because the initiative has been*

taken away from the learner and the construction no longer makes personal sense. (Fisher, J., 1996. p7)

For young children to be successful learners, connections must be made *between* their learning experiences. Traditionally, good Early Years practice is seen to be promoting this through an understanding of how children learn and the setting up of appropriate environments (Bruce, 1987; Nutbrown, 1999). This is sometimes termed 'developmentally appropriate practice' (Bredekamp, 1991). In America the National Association for the Education of Young Children defined this practice as requiring

> *...that teachers integrate the many dimensions of their knowledge base. They must know about child development and the implications of this knowledge for how to teach, the content of the curriculum – what to teach and when – how to assess what children have learned, and how to adapt curriculum and instruction to children's individual strengths, needs and interests.* (NAEYC, 1996)

Martin Woodhead refined the term to 'Practice appropriate to the context of early development' or PACED (Woodhead, 1996. p59). His emphasis is more specific, as the word 'context' suggests a more wide ranging approach in which practitioners will utilise and make best use of the available situation.

How then do recent initiatives and their effect upon learning and teaching stand up against this definition?

The Foundation Stage: implementation

The introduction of the Foundation Stage and the development of guidance that supports it (QCA, 2000) were hailed by many as a positive step for the education of children under five. The *Times Educational Supplement* carried an article which presented the Stage as 'brand new' – as if it had been borne out of nothing and with no recognition of existing practices and local strategies which informed its development:

> *The new foundation stage, which enshrines a play-based curriculum for three-to five-year-olds, came into force last September. Although the first children taught under the new system will be entering Year 1 next term, the detail and practice still seem largely a mystery to many infant and junior teachers. The Government has spent £13m nationally on early years co-ordinators to help with methodology and deal with queries. One of their challenges is to explain the significance of the changes for the whole school.* (TES Primary magazine, July/August, 2001)

How far this development was 'new' and the extent to which it was welcomed is open to question. Four and five year olds in school were no longer to be seen as part of Key Stage One (5-7 year olds) but taught in a distinct organisational phase for children aged from three years to five + (the end of the reception class year). Consequently children might begin their Foundation Stage in a nursery or play-group or with a childminder and transfer to a reception class at the start of the year in which they became four years old. This was seen as a somewhat radical organisational change:

> The establishment of a Foundation Stage is a significant landmark in funded education in England. For the first time it gives this very important stage of education a distinct identity. (QCA, 2000.p3)

This statement deserves some attention for, whilst official recognition of early learning is important, the language used above reinforces some important preconceptions:

- There is an implicit assumption that prior to the 'establishment of a Foundation Stage', the early years did not have a 'distinct identity', yet practitioners and local authorities have always regarded work with under fives as a distinct phase.

- By creating and naming a 'stage' designed to be an introduction to Key Stage 1, the government has reinforced a subject driven curriculum, and identified specific teaching and learning requirements at an even earlier age.

- The word 'education' is used twice. No-one would dispute that learning is important, and it is widely accepted that many children are learning all the time – in and outside of organised learning groups. To put early learning in a category as a 'stage of education' carries with it the ideas mentioned above. Teachers of young children are in the business of *scaffolding and supporting* children as they learn. If the word 'learning' were substituted for 'education' it would suggest more of an interactive process. The early years are a 'very important stage' of learning. The word education here seems to imply instruction or schooling especially when linked to the word funded. This in turn conjures up an image of a rigid and prescriptive curriculum that can quantifiably justify funding (presumably by producing results on paper). Accountability is a good thing, but the methods by which early education is justified need to be examined (Nutbrown, 1998).

The Foundation Stage Guidance (QCA, 2000) does not necessarily need to be resisted, but it should be challenged and questioned with regard to its interpretation, appropriate delivery and underlying expectations. What lies behind it? The document itself can be a powerful influence on the structure of planning, the content of curriculum and teaching styles in reception classes.

That the government has recognised good Early Years practice and the need to create structures to promote some continuity to provision is a positive policy development. There is now, in England and Wales, official recognition that young children do not learn best in formally taught lessons, and that the Key Stage 1 curriculum requires solid underpinning with a range of fundamental experiences which help children to develop socially, emotionally, physically and creatively. Whilst literacy and numeracy are important, they cannot be readily learnt if the child is not equipped with other more basic skills and the disposition to learn. This sort of development, which often happens so naturally at home, has become stifled in many settings by the pressures of the National Curriculum (Jenkinson, 2001).

The establishment of the Foundation Stage might have brought a sigh of relief from Early Years practitioners in infant and primary schools who had struggled to work with and adapt inappropriate expectations of a rigid curriculum based primarily on the needs of older children. For example, the *Literacy Hour* and the *Daily Maths Lesson* need no longer be enforced since government guidance had recognised that young children do not learn in compartments and that play has an educational value. Teaching is defined in the Foundation Stage guidance as

...systematically helping children to learn so that they are helped to make connections in their learning and are actively led forward, as well as helped to reflect on what they have already learnt.

...Practitioners teach children in many ways. The different ways to teach may be selected at the planning stage or may be a perceptive response to what children do or say.

...The strategies used in learning and teaching should vary and should be adapted to suit the needs of the child.

(QCA, 2000 p22)

Thus the Foundation Stage guidance resonates with sound theory about how young children learn. This should eliminate misplaced policy initiatives or inappropriate classroom practice, but any guidance depends for its success on the people who put it into practice and such practitioners were already in the midst of implementing several other new policy initiatives which affected pedagogy.

The Foundation Stage: policy influences

There has long been concern about the admission of four year olds to school and the appropriateness of curriculum and expectations (Cleave and Brown, 1991). The changes in government policy for England and Wales offered the hope of clarification and perhaps parity of experience for young children. Fisher's definition (see page 13) summarises what could be expected in a Foundation Stage for 3-5+ year old children. However, as the guidance spans a wide spectrum of provision and must identify good practice and ways of accounting for the effectiveness of that practice.

It is perhaps surprising that recognition of a Foundation Stage for learning was not established until 2000. Much work preceded it, such as the multidisciplinary '*Quality in Diversity*', (ECEF, 1998) which promoted the importance of understanding early childhood and expressed concern that

...developments within the wider education system – in relation to curriculum, assessment, inspection and education of teachers – have not been built either on an understanding of how young children learn or on existing best practice in early childhood settings. (Early Childhood Education Forum, 1998 p2)

There is still huge diversity in understanding the early years at school and two different agendas often compete: the needs of the child and 'targets' and accountability. The two need not necessarily be in opposition but the reality is that they often are. Historically, the Early Years have always been perceived as the poor relation of state education (largely because of its non-statutory status) but much work has been done at a policy level to define quality provision and practice and these indicate a policy shift throughout the 1990s. At least four major reports have pronounced on the nature of quality provision for the educational needs of young children: *The Education of Children Under Five* (HMI report, DES, 1989), *Starting with Quality,* (Rumbold Report, DES, 1990), *Learning to Succeed* (National Commission on Education, 1993) and *Start Right: The Importance of Early Learning* (Royal Society of Arts, Ball, 1994). Drawing on these various policy related reports, Fisher identified 'quality indicators', the most relevant to this discussion being:

> **An appropriate curriculum** planned to develop the whole child, providing experiences relevant to child's *current* needs. Additionally, policy documents state that children under five are not subject to the National Curriculum but should have a curriculum not planned in subjects but based upon *areas of learning.*
>
> **Periods of time for sustained self-initiated activity** where children have the opportunity to make choices and decisions. Additionally, children should not be interrupted by the fixed timetable (primary assemblies, for example are not compulsory for children under five) and continual access to an outdoor area for learning is important ('playtime' is not necessary for children under five in these circumstances).
>
> **Appropriately trained and experienced educators with a knowledge of child development.** This means that teachers should be appropriately trained for the age/year group. Teachers should have acquired further training and/or qualifications in early childhood education and other staff should have appropriate qualifications for working with young children.
>
> **Collaborative planning based on systematic observation of children in all areas of development.** This requires systematic observation by all adults who work with the child (e.g. teacher, nursery nurse, Learning Support Assistant, parent). It also requires collaborative planning by all those involved in the observation, systems which allow observations to be incorporated into formative records which inform planning, and assessments of both teacher-initiated and self-chosen activities.
>
> (Adapted from Fisher, 1996 pp160-161)

As most children in England and Wales enter primary school at the age of four instead of five, these indicators become crucial. Whilst it is accepted that nursery provision caters appropriately for the needs of children under five, this is not necessarily the case for all reception classes. There are many questions: Should there be a subject-based curriculum? Would the importance of play be lost?

What are the social aims for children? Government policy literature, certainly until 1996, emphasised what was appropriate for the needs of the children – despite the pressures of the National Curriculum introduced in September 1989. Two policy developments heralded the start of a change in emphasis: *Desirable Outcomes for Children's Learning'* (criteria for inspection to be used to allocate funding to providers) and Baseline Assessment (a national requirement to assess all children within seven weeks of beginning school). *Desirable Outcomes for Children's Learning* (SCAA, 1996), 'radically altered the responsibilities of practitioners and providers', and 'challenged practitioners to reconcile their old and new responsibilities' (Blenkin and Kelly, 1997 p35). The Desirable Outcomes gave specific targets that were to be met, thus ending the confusion about whether reception children who were not yet five should follow the National Curriculum, and established detailed 'goals for learning for children by the time they enter compulsory education', which is the term after their fifth birthday (SCAA, 1996 p1).

Baseline Assessment was the inevitable consequence of the Desirable Learning Outcomes; from September 1998 all children were to be assessed after their first seven weeks in the reception class. Baseline assessment was already widely used as a way of gauging the capabilities of children on entry, but change in policy made such assessments a requirement from September 1998. The rationale behind this was twofold: teachers needed to understand the children on entry to school, and managers and policy makers wanted data to enable accountability.

These two initiatives resulted in what could be seen as a new era in state funded Early Childhood Education. There was now a curriculum which, by way of justification, was shown to link directly with the National Curriculum. There was also testing which, just as in later Key Stages, would allow for calculation of how much 'value' had been 'added' by the end school. These changes placed significant pressure on reception teachers during children's first seven weeks of school as they tried to meet the needs of children new to their classes and administer the nationally required assessments. This happened despite the stated desirability that:

Children feel secure, valued and confident and develop a sense of achievement through learning which is a pleasurable and rewarding experience... (SCAA, 1996 p6)

But the pressure did not end with the establishment of Desirable Learning Outcomes and the imposition of Baseline Assessment. The National Literacy Strategy launched in 1998 set out 'teaching objectives for Reception to Year 6 to enable pupils to become fully literate'. It also gave 'guidance on the literacy hour in which this teaching will take place' (DFEE, 1998 p2) and advice about how to manage the literacy hour within a reception class in the context of the Desirable Learning Outcomes.

The central issue here is whether teaching literacy to such young children in a structured hour is more effective than teaching it throughout the day, as previously, but the policy on this is clear:

Teachers should plan to introduce a full Literacy Hour as soon as possible and, at the very latest, by the end of the term before children move into Year 1. (DFEE, 1998 p2)

There is no rationale for this statement which seems to run counter to much of what we knew about learning, and literacy learning in particular (Hall, 1982; Hannon and Nutbrown, 1997).

Fisher argues that, in a reception class,

Teacher-intensive, teacher-initiated and child-initiated activities should all be of value to the teacher and to the children, and should all be planned for specific learning purposes. (Fisher, 1996 p60)

Some child-initiated activities cannot be planned for but, where appropriate, they should be used by the teacher to enhance motivated learning. In order that all these activities should be accorded equal status, Fisher argues that they should be:

...happening at the same time as each other, not one always preceding the others because it is seen by the teacher as being more important. (p60)

The expectations of the Literacy Strategy do not allow for this possibility. It must be acknowledged that many of the practices promoted in the *Literacy Hour* were drawn from models of effective practice. But the notion of an hour was unworkable, since cramming a range of activities end-to-end within an hour exhausted young children and their teachers and went against the grain of literacy as an all pervasive curriculum element.

Less than a year later, March 1999, saw a further initiative. The National Numeracy Strategy took into account the Early Learning Goals (QCA, 2000) and the Foundation Stage but retained the practice of discrete teaching time, with the view that children must be prepared by the end of Reception, 'for the dedicated mathematics lesson of about 45 minutes that will be part of each day in Year 1' (DfEE, 1999 p27). To prepare the children they should be helped to learn 'how to listen, how to show and talk about what they have been doing in front of other children, how to find and use the equipment that they need, how to take turns, and so on' ((DfEE, 1999 p27). Reception teachers would recognise these as established features of good early years practice.

Conclusion

In summary, the four initiatives since 1999 led Reception teachers to move towards a subject led curriculum for 4 and 5 year old children and it was against this policy background that the Foundation Stage (QCA, 2000) was introduced. This chapter has reviewed the key policy developments as they have taken effect in reception classes in England and Wales since 1996. There can be little doubt that this phase of education was the subject of major policy developments and intense public pressure at the turn of the century. It will be interesting to see whether the Early Learning Goals and the Foundation Stage Guidance will undergo further review and change as they 'bed-down' in the first decade of the 21st century. The evidence would suggest that this should happen, as they are based upon a subject-specific method of teaching which is open to misinterpretation. In February 2002, the government concluded that it no longer needed to prioritise Early Childhood Education. As long as this is the case, it remains with us, as practitioners and researchers, to ensure that good early years practice is promoted and strengthened.

References

Ball, C. (1994) *Start Right: The Importance of Early Learning* London: Royal Society of Arts

Blenkin, G.M and Kelly, A.V. (1997) *Principles into Practice in Early Childhood Education* London: Paul Chapman Publishing

Bredekamp, S. (1991) *Developmentally Appropriate Practice* New York: NAYEC

Bruce, T. (1987) *Early Childhood Education* London: Hodder and Stoughton

Cleave, S. and Brown, S. (1991) *Early to School: Four year olds in infant classes* Windsor: NFER-Nelson

DES (1989) *Education of Children Under Five* London: HMSO

DES (1990) *Starting with Quality* London: HMSO

DfEE (1998) *The National Literacy Strategy* London: DfEE

DfEE (1999) *The National Numeracy Strategy* London: DfEE

Early Childhood Education Forum (1998) *Quality in Diversity* London: National Children's Bureau

Fisher, J. (1996) *Starting from the Child?* Buckingham: Open University Press

Hall, N. (1982) *The Emergence of Literacy* London: Hodder and Stoughton

Hannon, P. and Nutbrown, C (1997) *Preparing for Early Literacy Development with Parents: a professional development manual* Nottingham/ Sheffield: NES ARNOLD/ REAL Project

Jenkinson, S. (2001) *The Genius of Play* Stroud: Hawthorn Press

NAYEC (1996) *Guidelines for decisions about developmentally appropriate practice* On-line http:www.nayec.org/about/position/dap4.htm

National Commission on Education (1993) *Learning to Succeed* London: Heinemann

Nutbrown, C. (1999) *Threads of Thinking: young children learning and the role of early education* London: Paul Chapman Publishing

Nutbrown, C. ((1998) Early Assessment: examining the baselines *Early Education* 19, 1, 50-61

QCA (2000) *Curriculum Guidance for the Foundation Stage* London: QCA

SCAA (1996) *Desirable Outcomes for Children's Learning* London: DfEE/SCAA

Woodhead, M. (1996) *In Search of the Rainbow* Netherlands: Bernard van Leer Foundation

3

Assessing the future: Baseline Assessment

Di Chilvers

Assessment is a process that must enrich their lives, their learning and development. Assessment must work for children. (Drummond, 1995 p13)

Introduction

The publication in 2000 of the *Curriculum Guidance for the Foundation Stage* (QCA/DfEE., 2000) created an ambiguous future for Baseline Assessment, raising the questions: Where will *Baseline Assessment* 'fit' now and what should it look like? This chapter reports a small scale study which examined the views of early years practitioners across England and Wales. The findings suggest that appropriate assessment of young children includes an emphasis on observation and takes place at key points in the Foundation Stage. These conclusions are not necessarily in harmony with government policy on the baseline assessment of young children but they do accord with much recent research.

Aims of the Study

Whilst attention has been paid to the introduction of the Foundation Stage (QCA, 2000), the issue of how this should affect Baseline Assessment was 'left for later discussion'. Despite recommendations from practitioners, professional organisations and the academy that *Baseline Assessment* should be reviewed as part of this key initiative decisions about the future of Baseline Assessment were not made in 2000 and children continued to be assessed within seven weeks of entry to school (often at around their fourth birthday) even

23

though this was in the middle of the new *Foundation Stage* (3-5 years). No other Key Stage has a *required and reported* assessment at the mid-point.

The professional opinions of a range of early years practitioners are central to this study of Baseline Assessment and the Foundation Stage so a small scale study was carried out within this policy context to:

- consult early years practitioners for their views on the future of Baseline Assessment in light of the Foundation Stage

- ascertain early years practitioner's views of when Baseline Assessment should be administered and what it should involve

- establish current practice in terms of assessment

- consider the use of observation to make assessments and how this could influence the future of Baseline Assessment

Questionnaires were sent out to members of Early Education (formerly the British Association for Early Childhood Education) across the country and it was also posted on the Early Education web site.

This small scale study is modest in its scope, based as it is on the views of a small number of early years practitioners, all with an understanding of good practice and pedagogy in the early years.

There are three main issues to consider:

- the recent history of Baseline Assessment

- recent practice in assessment and the introduction of the Foundation Stage (QCA, 2000)

- alternative approaches to assessment in the Foundation Stage

The recent history of Baseline Assessment
Proposals for the introduction of Baseline Assessment were published in September 1996 (SCAA) and it became a legal requirement in September 1998 (Education Act 1997), but assessment in the early years was not a new phemonenon. Assessment has always been part of the teachers' role, enabling them to plan for children's learn-

ing and monitor their progress (Blenkin and Kelly, 1992). Assessments have, for example, been used to identify children with Special Educational Needs and pro-actively to address the individual learning needs of all children. This was the historical root of Baseline Assessment, where individual children's needs were identified, and future progress planned for, within the school environment.

The late 1980s and early 1990s saw an increase in staff development sessions related to recording achievement and assessing children's learning. Professional development and training seemed dominated by the need to develop and implement assessments in the early years. '*All About Me*', a personal profile for each child (Wolfendale, 1990) was regarded as the way forward in recording the personal history and progress of young children. This led to the nation-wide production of scrapbooks, children's portfolios and records of achievement. But such developments were to be shortlived as pressures of the National Curriculum (DES, 1989) took hold and Standard Assessment Tests were introduced to measure children's achievements at the end of Key Stage 1. The policy of using measures of children's achievements to demonstrate the rise in educational standards was being introduced but there was a problem in measuring success at the end of Key Stage 1, as Lindsay and Desforges (1998, p5) point out:

> At the end of Key Stages 2 and 3 the results at the end of the previous key stage can be used to measure progress, but this is not possible for Key Stage 1 unless Baseline Assessment is introduced for all five year old pupils as they enter infant school.

So the notion of *value-added* was created both to account for the child's progress from the beginning of their school life, and to be measured by means of a baseline assessment within the first seven weeks of children entering school, regardless of their age. Since 1998 the implementation of Baseline Assessment has caused much concern; the draft proposals (SCAA, 1996) led to target driven assessments and the emphasis of measurement over achievements.

Baseline Assessment has been described as a way of understanding what children know and can do in order to plan and provide 'learning activities that match the child's needs' (SCAA, 1996 p4). As long as a scheme followed the key principles of the National Framework

(SCAA, 1996 p12) and was approved by SCAA, schools could choose which assessment scheme they used. Over 90 schemes received the approval of the Schools Curriculum and Assessment Authority. This was a small victory for diversity but did little to address the concerns outlined by Lindsay and Desforges (1998).

Two key purposes of Baseline Assessment were stated in government documentation:

- *to provide information to help teachers plan effectively to meet children's individual learning needs*

and

- *to measure children's attainment, using one or more numerical outcomes which can be used in later value-added analyses of children's progress.*

(SCAA, 1997 p3)

Initial proposals for Baseline Assessment in 1996 emphasised the former of these two purposes (SCAA, 1996 p6) and the importance of assessment processes which would not overly disrupt teaching. But within four years (by 2000) the emphasis of Baseline Assessment had effectively changed to a measure of value-addedness and with this came serious implications for the education of young children. Drummond (1995) had warned of this:

> *...the term 'assessment' has come to suggest an objective, mechanical process of measurement. It suggests checklists, precision, explicit criteria, incontrovertible facts and figures.* (p13)

In 1996 SCAA stated that the primary role of assessment was to 'enhance children's learning' and *after that* to 'measure a child's attainment so that future progress can be identified and monitored' (SCAA, 1996 p7). Since 2000 these two key purposes have been in direct conflict; assessment for promoting a child's development and learning being manipulated into a tool for measuring their progress against national targets and outcomes (Drummond, 1995; Nutbrown, 1998, 1999).

Recent practice of assessment and the introduction of the Foundation Stage

Early years practitioners have made assessments of children for many years. When practitioners talk to parents and carers about their child before they enter nursery provision, they are gaining knowledge of that child as a person and as a learner in their own right. Edgington (1998) refers to staff 'collecting information' from parents before the child enters the provision suggesting that such information forms a life history and provides a picture of the development of the child, in a way which acknowledges that the child is *already* a learner and has at least three years of previous learning before joining a nursery.

Building on children's previous knowledge and experience and making sure that new learning is matched to previous learning is established Early Years practice. Accordingly, Baseline Assessment could be a useful way of establishing an understanding of a child's present knowledge and capabilities but would not offer a measure of the value-added According to the Effective Provision of Pre-School Education Project, it is:

> essential to have accurate baseline data about children's cognitive attainments and details of their social and behavioural development, so that subsequent progress and development can be measured. (EPPE, 2000 p3-4)

Many early years practitioners would not admit to undertaking a baseline assessment but they would probably describe their practice of taking an what they called an *entry profile or questionnaire for parents*, as Edgington notes:

> Although 'to monitor progress' is one of their reasons for record-keeping, few teachers feel comfortable with the idea of measuring children's attainment and giving numerical scores which can be used in later value added analysis of children's progress. (Edgington, 1998 p122)

Many practitioners are reluctant to use terms such as *measuring attainment* because it suggests target driven assessment and pressure to prepare children for Key Stage 1. Downward pressures have threatened early years teaching since the National Curriculum was introduced in 1989, the effect being a curriculum with a focus on what is to be assessed rather than the potential breadth of children's learning (Blenkin and Kelly, 1992).Target driven assessment does not show respect for children as learners; Drummond calls this 'dead-end' assessment (see Lindsey and Desforges, 1998).

The introduction of the Foundation Stage (QCA) in September 2000 brought a welcome relief from the downward pressure of the

National Curriculum and its related assessment. Where practitioners interpreted its principles and intentions alongside established good early years practice, this provided what we could call a concrete lintel to resist downward pressure and establish the Foundation Stage as a period of educare in its own right. The Guidance (QCA, 2000) discussed in detail the function and practice of assessment for young children. Baseline Assessment or measuring the child's achievements to the learning goals is not mentioned but it is acknowledged that some children will reach the goals at the end of the Foundation Stage while others will not (QCA, 2000 p17, 26). However, there is a huge and evident danger here that inexperienced practitioners might take the 'stepping stones' and the 'goals' and use them as check-lists styled assessments – a point raised by Edgington:

> ...ticking off attainment may seem attractively simple but, as many teachers have discovered, does not take into account the wonderful spontaneity or creativity of young children. Nor does it allow for the child who, in using materials or expressing ideas in unexpected ways, demonstrates levels of thinking way beyond our expectations. (Edgington, 1998 p120)

It is important to consider the Curriculum Guidance for the Foundation Stage on the assessment of children's learning:

- the process of assessment begins before the child joins the setting with 'practitioners listening to parents' accounts of their child's development and noting any concerns'

- working in partnership with parents/carers in the '...assessment and planning process' is important

- assessments should be used not only in terms of the children and their development but to '...evaluate the quality of the provision and (to identify) practitioners' training needs'

- assessment should serve several purposes, such as giving an 'insight into children's interests, achievements and possible difficulties in their learning'

- assessments which can either be planned for or spontaneous, arising out of the child's self-initiated play, should be used

- it is important to use assessments to inform and guide planning, 'identifying the next step in children's learning to plan how to help children make progress' (QCA, 2000 p 8 and 24)

This final point has placed some emphasis on early years practitioners knowing about how children develop and how they learn best. Indeed the guidance stresses the need for practitioners to have a knowledge of child development and children's learning in order to make experiences in the Foundation Stage appropriate to the particular needs of the individual.

> Where practitioners are clear about what children know, the skills they have developed, the attitudes they have towards learning and the interests they have, they can plan how best to take the learning and teaching forward. (QCA, 2000 p24)

Alternative approaches to assessment in the Foundation Stage

Baseline Assessment and its place in early education are therefore open to criticism. So what alternative might be proposed? A more appropriate way of assessing young children's learning is the use of observation (Drummond, 1995; Drummond and Nutbrown, 1996; Edgington, 1998; Fisher, 1996; Nutbrown,1998, 1999; QCA, 2000). This approach demonstrates a return to the skilful observation of children during their play by practitioners who can recognise what they are doing, interpret this into the assessment of what the child is learning/understanding and inform the planning of teaching to take a child's learning forward. Or

> ...the way in which, in our everyday practice, we observe children's learning, strive to understand it, and then put our understanding to good use. (Drummond, 1995)

Observation of children during their play or at any other time can tell us so much more about the child as a whole person and a whole learner than restricting our view of them and their learning to narrow, adult-led targets and outcomes. So much more can be gleaned from watching children as they demonstrate their huge capacity and motivation to find out and then comparing what we have observed to what we know about child development and children as learners. In one short sequence of events, the practitioner can identify the child's attitudes and dispositions towards learning, reflect on previous learning and propose the development of the child's future learning.

> Observation and assessment are the processes by which we can both establish the progress that has already been made, and explore the future, the learning that is yet to come. (Drummond and Nutbrown, 1996 p105)

Using observation as a method of assessment can create a much broader picture of the child and a more secure baseline from which to work. Opposing views will bring into play the time factor, provoking insistence that there isn't the time to make such observations of children and their learning. But making the time for respectful observation and assessment of children's learning is a realistic possibility and this is now positively encouraged in official policy documentation (QCA, 2000).

Methodology of the study

A short questionnaire was designed to collect general details of the respondents' professional development and experience and their understanding of Baseline Assessment. Questionnaires as a method of gathering research can restrict the respondent's answer to the space provided, leading to answers which lack depth and are closed to the possibility of further questioning. They also rely heavily on the motivation of the respondent to return it. However, if questions are carefully constructed and answered by willing and honest respondents, questionnaires can focus the respondents' thinking and provide the researcher with clear straightforward responses to evaluate.

This study focuses on a sample of 20 questionnaires drawn from a pool of 93 volunteer returns. These were chosen to because they represented a range of perspectives of early years professionals in a variety of locations around the UK. Fifteen of the 20 responses were from providers who were directly linked in some way to a Local Education Authority.

Analysis and findings

Since the introduction of the Foundation Stage (QCA, 2000) has finally led to a more streamlined approach to transition from nursery to key stage 1, reception class children are no longer drifting between desirable outcomes and key stages, but gathered into the Foundation Stage with a clear curriculum pathway. Therefore the responses to the question of when Baseline Assessment should take place is perhaps predictable; thirteen respondents said that Baseline Assessment should take place at the end of the Foundation stage, four suggested that it should take place at the beginning of the

Foundation Stage and two suggested that it should be located at the mid-way point (see Table 1).

Table 1: When should Baseline Assessment take place?

In the light of the introduction of the Foundation Stage where do you see 'Baseline Assessment'?	Responses (n=20)
At the end of the Foundation Stage	10
At the beginning of Key Stage 1	3
Prior to entry to nursery provision	4
At the beginning of the Reception Year for all children	2
Not sure	1

Questionnaire responses illuminate the argument for assessment at the start of Key Stage 1:

- as an entry profile for Key Stage 1 rather than a Foundation Stage 'SAT'

- the beginning of year 1 is the only point at which all children are in the same academic cohort and of statutory school age

- occurring once the child is fully settled into Key Stage 1, not six weeks into induction.

There has been an assumption that Baseline Assessment only occurs when children enter formal schooling and is used primarily as a tool for the measurement of value-added and child/teacher performance (see, for example Lindsay and Desforges, 1998). Yet early years practitioners have long been involved in what Fisher (1996) terms 'conversations' or discussions with parents and carers who really know their child, about the children's earlier progress and development. This has often formed the first Baseline Assessment and the beginning of an entry profile of the child from which practitioners built on what children already know and can do (QCA, 2000 p11). In the questionnaire survey which forms the basis of this chapter, four out of 20 practitioners suggested making some kind of assessment of the child on entry to nursery, so as to get to know them as soon as possible. They said:

- a true Baseline Assessment would take place on entry to nursery

- we need to look at nursery children... in the early weeks

If Baseline Assessment came at the *end* of the Foundation Stage or the beginning of Key Stage 1, it would form a means of monitoring children's progress and planning for the next period of their education. It would make sense to include in this some previously recorded entry information about a child at an earlier stage in order to show continuity in their education and learning. Respondents were also asked what constitutes a 'true baseline' and if they carried out such assessments before entry to the Foundation Stage (i.e. at 3 years old). Of the 20, eleven said they did and eight that they did not (the remaining respondent said the question did not apply to her context).

Some respondents clarified their answer to the question *Are the children in your setting assessed before entry to the Foundation Stage?* by replying:

- No – unless you count the parent questionnaire completed at induction day

- No – but we do a language sample

- Yes – against our better judgement

It is possible to interpret the two examples of 'no' responses as affirmative – given the clarification provided and depending on how Baseline Assessment is defined. Practitioners in the survey were making Baseline Assessments before children entered the Foundation Stage but they did not call it an 'assessment'. Practitioners referred to assessment in other ways and tended to see it not as a way of measuring value added but as something more meaningful in itself, that would benefit the children and their individual progress. This is evident in the following explanations about when they assessed children and how:

- in the last half term before leaving for school with the key worker, evidence gathered together from profile of achievement, discussed as a whole staff

- through their statement of educational needs

- information gathered from home visits plus observation and assessments, ongoing to inform planning for each child. Final summary transfer form completed and shared with parents and reception teacher, but without numerical scores

- parents complete an assessment form and individual child record form. Staff observe and record the child's competences across the learning areas

- children with medical needs e.g. Cerebral Palsy, Downs Syndrome, have multi-assessments

- no formal assessments made but detailed records and observations are passed from feeder playgroups which are referred to, and passed on, on transfer to make sure baselines are 'fair'

- starting to use ASPECTS on an individual basis during the child's first three weeks

- assessed in nursery from entry, recorded on profile sheet which is in line with assessments in school and accompanies the child on transfer. Work closely with the Reception teacher.

Most of the practitioners in this survey were involved in making a Baseline Assessment of children as they entered the Foundation Stage at the age of three. This often involved discussions or 'conversations' (Fisher, 1996) with parents/carers as well as with educators in previous settings. Which suggests that providers seek to find out about the context of the child's life and previous learning from the people who know them best. Observation of children is also identified by many practitioners as a key component of their assessments and in some cases this is used to plan future teaching. Such assessments are passed on during transition from Foundation Stage to Key Stage 1.

There seems to be a reluctance amongst early years educators to describe their usual practice of making entry profiles and discussing children's previous progress with their parents as a Baseline Assessment. Arguably, though, this is what they are doing. The difference is in the purpose for doing it (Nutbrown, 1997). The focus is firmly on assessment of the child to inform planning which in turn provides learning opportunities appropriate and relevant to the child (QCA, 2000; Nutbrown, 2001).

Practitioners stated what they felt baseline assessment should include:

- the child's personal, social and emotional development
- observation of the child by the practitioner/parent carer
- aspects of literacy and numeracy (linked to the strategies)
- the six *areas of learning*
- assessment of skills e.g.practical skills such as cutting, gross motor skills
- English as an Additional Language
- general language development
- teacher assessment of formal tasks
- an overall picture of the child – a profile
- dispositions to learning e.g. concentration, perseverance, well-being

Though this list suggests a wide variation in what constitutes a Baseline Assessment, some suggestion of priorities emerges. For example, ten of the twenty respondents placed assessment of personal, social and emotional development as a priority. Why should this be? Is it because of the social nature of early education or is it an acknowledgement that the emotional well-being of the child is crucial to their ability to learn (Nutbrown, 1998; QCA, 2000; Dyer in this volume).

The place of observation in Baseline Assessment is highlighted by nine respondents, who referred to how this should be used in assessment of the child. One respondent stressed the need to make 'contextualised learning assessments' based on observations of children during their play. This was the only response which referred directly to observing children during their play and making assessments from that, and it is interesting to note the lack of reference to play in the responses, perhaps indicating how play and assessment have become polarised in the thinking of some early years practitioners. Observation is frequently undervalued as a 'tool' for assessment, despite continued argument for its place as *the* primary assessment tool in the early years (Nutbrown, 2001). The introduction of the Foundation Stage in September 2000 endorsed the use of observation as a method of assessment with comments such as:

> Practitioners must be able to observe and respond appropriately to children. (QCA, 2000 p11 and 24)

Responses which refer to the literacy and numeracy strategies and the 'six areas of learning' (QCA, 2000) as being a part of Baseline Assessment is not surprising. This is somewhat disconcerting as the drive to measure outcomes and turn 'stepping stones' (QCA, 2000) into 'targets' suggests the threat of misinterpretation of the intended pedagogy of the Foundation Stage. One wonders how the balance might be tipped in order to ensure that the all round development of children is valued and assessed with assessments which take in to account children's dispositions for learning and Baseline Assessments which give an overall picture of each child's capabilities.

Professional opinion seems to support the retiming of Baseline Assessment at the end of the Foundation Stage. However, this risks making Baseline Assessment an end of stage SAT for five year olds (*Times Educational Supplement* 20/10/2000). Ideally, the most appropriate place for this assessment is at the beginning of Key Stage 1, where it could be used as an entry profile into that Key Stage. There may be more evidence to support this view when the longitudinal study from the EPPE Project (Sammons *et al.*) is reported in 2003.

As for what Baseline Assessment should look 'like', research and professional judgement concur that what is required is assessment which will give a broader and fuller picture of each child's progress and enable them to move forward in their learning at a pace which is appropriate for them so that they truly understand the process of that learning:

> Assessment is a process that must enrich their lives, their learning and development. Assessment must work for children. (Drummond, 1995 p13)

This is not the easy path to take and requires well trained and competent early years practitioners. It takes more time, but this kind of assessment is actually more powerful and meaningful, because it tells the practitioner so much more about the child's development and how they are learning. It is not assessment for management and accountability but it is assessment for teaching and learning (Nutbrown, 1999).

The future and nature of Baseline Assessment is cause for great concern, but as the new Foundation Stage Profile indicates a move towards observation-based assessment at this point (DfES, 2002). The Curriculum Guidance for the Foundation Stage (QCA, 2000) emphasised an approach to assessment which values the way young children learn encourages observation of children to identify where they are in their development and use this information to inform planning and develop the curriculum. However, Foundation Stage practitioners should be aware of the danger of interpreting the *Curriculum Guidance* (QCA, 2000) into a numerical baseline measure which devalues the importance of the Foundation Stage Profile.

This chapter has reported a small-scale enquiry into the nature and practices of Baseline Assessment, in an attempt to anticipate its future. Further research is required into alternative approaches to formal Baseline Assessments and what they should include but, perhaps more importantly, policy makers should monitor the introduction of the Foundation Stage Profile from September 2002 – and ensure its priority over more narrow, numerically-based assessment in the early years.

References

Blenkin, G.M. and Kelly, A.V. (Eds) (1992) *Assessment in Early Childhood Education* London: Paul Chapman Publishing

Drummond, M.J. (1995) *Assessing Children's Learning* London: David Fulton

Drummond, M.J. and Nutbrown C. (1996) 'Observing and Assessing Young Children' in Pugh.G (Ed) *Contemporary Issues in the Early Years: Working Collaboratively for Children* (Second Edition), London: Paul Chapman Publishing and National Children's Bureau

Early Education: ONLINE:www.early-education.org.uk

Early Years Curriculum Group. (1998) *Positive Action for the Early Years: Action Paper 4: Baseline Assessment* Early Years Curriculum Group

Edgington, M. (1998) *The Nursery Teacher in Action: Teaching 3,4 and 5 Year Olds* (Second Edition), London: Paul Chapman Publishing

Fisher, J. (1996) *Starting from the Child? Teaching and Learning from 4 to 8* Buckingham: Open University Press

Hurst, V. and Lally, M. (1992) 'Assessment and the National Curriculum' in Blenkin, G.M. and Kelly, A.V. (Eds) *Assessment in Early Childhood Education* London: Paul Chapman Publishing

Lally, M. and Hurst,V. (1992) 'Assessment in Nursery Education: A Review of Approaches' in Blenkin, G.M. and Kelly, A.V. (Ed) *Assessment in Early Childhood Education* London: Paul Chapman Publishing

Lindsay, G. and Desforges, M. (1998) *Baseline Assessment: Practice, Problems and Possibilities* London: David Fulton

Nutbrown, C. (1998) 'Early Assessment-Examining the Baselines' *Early Years* Vol 19, No.1, pp50-61

Nutbrown, C. (1999) 'Baseline Assessment of Writing – the need for reconsideration' *Journal of Research in Reading*, Vol 22, Issue 1, pp37-44

Qualifications and Curriculum Authority and Department for Education and Employment (2000) *Curriculum Guidance for the Foundation Stage* London: Qualifications and Curriculum Authority

Sainsbury, M. (1998) *Making Sense of Baseline Assessment* London: Hodder and Stoughton

Sammons, P., Sylva, K., Melhuish, E., Siraj-Blatchford, I., Taggart, B., Smees, R., Dobson, A., Jeavons, M., Lewis, K., Morahan, M , Sadler, S. (1999) *Technical Paper 2: Characteristics of the Effective Provision of Pre-School Education (EPPE) Project* Institute of Education, University of London

School Curriculum and Assessment Authority (1996) *Baseline Assessment: Draft Proposals* Middlesex: SCAA

School Curriculum and Assessment Authority (1997) *Baseline Assessment: Information for Schools* London: SCAA

Sylva, K., Melhuish, E., Sammons, P., Siraj-Blatchford, I. (September 2000) *The EPPE Symposium at The British Educational Research Association Annual Conference* (pp1-10) ONLINE:http://www.ioe.ac.uk/cdl/eppe

Wolfendale, S. (1990) *All About Me* Nottingham: NES-Arnold

Note: a version of this chapter was presented at the Annual Conference of the British Association for Early Childhood Education, London, in November 2000

4

Practice and policy for assessment in early childhood settings

Julie Bravery

Introduction

Assessment *'opens our eyes to the astonishing capacity of young children to learn'* (Drummond and Nutbrown 1992, p88). It helps practitioners to understand what they see and enables us to learn from those who have gone before us such as Piaget and Donaldson. The immense capacity of children to learn places a huge responsibility on early years educators in providing the provision to extend and enrich this learning.

Assessment has a crucial role to play in achieving the highest quality provision for all young learners. Assessment allows us to judge whether the environment we provide supports children's development and also the planning of an appropriate curriculum to match each child's cognitive and personal development needs. Effective early childhood assessment allows us to value the role of parents as a child's first educator and value the expertise they can offer. For example, Athey found that *'the professionals identified schemas but, once identified, parents were able to give examples'* (Athey, 1990, p207). Assessment identifies for each individual the next steps that might take place in their learning and this is crucial if we are to support children in achieving their full potential as learners. Vygotsky called this 'the zone of proximal development', stating: *'I do not terminate my study at this point, but only begin it'* (Vygotsky, 1978 p85). Drummond and Nutbrown (1992) continue this theme:

> *Effective assessment is dynamic, not static, and can identify for the educator what the learner's next steps might be; assessment reveals learning potential as well as learning completed.* (p90).

Assessment is crucial to ensuring the best provision for children in our care. Effective assessment allows us to evaluate and enrich the curriculum we offer. Drummond and Pollard (1993) suggested that *'assessment is part of our daily practice in striving for quality'* (p13).

This chapter reports a study which investigated the extent to which practitioners used assessment within early childhood settings and what practices and policies influence the methods they used. This chapter considers the influence of assessment practices and policy on early childhood settings and reflects on the impact of the national curriculum Standard Assessment Tasks (SATs) and Baseline Assessment on early childhood assessment practices and policies. It establishes that both these policies have influenced the nature of assessment in the settings surveyed, often to the detriment of more fruitful and established early childhood assessment techniques such as observation. The chapter also considers whether approaches to assessment vary according to the type of setting a child attends. Interestingly, the study indicates that diversity in approaches across settings is limited.

Methodology

The research question at the centre of this study indicated a need for some form of quantifiable data collection. I wanted ultimately to be able to generalise about the current approaches to assessment within the early childhood setting using the data collected.

> The major strength of quantitative research designs is the potential for generalising the findings from the sample population to the larger population it represents. (MacNaughton et al, 2001 p113)

Clark's (1998) research on effective formative assessment in primary schools established clear principles for assessment, so I used these principles as a starting point in developing a questionnaire survey. The research was carried out collaboratively with a range of settings and judgements were made from the data collected, about the current assessment practices in early childhood settings and their appropriateness and effectiveness in ensuring a good quality early childhood curriculum for all children.

The questionnaire survey reached a wide range of participants, accumulating responses from a wide variety of settings to ensure all views were represented, thus targeting a cross-section of one hundred settings in Essex. The questionnaire is a widely used and useful instrument for collecting survey information, providing structured, often numerical data, and often being comparatively straightforward to analyse (Wilson and McLean, 1994). But there can be difficulties: time is needed to refine and develop the questionnaire and the detail of response may be limited, although Wilson and Mclean (1994) suggest this could equally be an attraction of this method.

Participants are likely to view completing a questionnaire with varying degrees of enthusiasm. Because of the time constraints already placed on practitioners working in early childhood settings the survey questionnaire needed to be straightforward and not too time-consuming. I therefore included questions requiring 'yes' or 'no' answers and a 'tick the box' approach. There were other advantages in this approach: it allowed me to collect and organise quantifiable data and it allowed practitioners to feel at ease with the answers they gave and not feel obliged to provide more complex written responses. Cohen *et al.* (2000) state

> The questionnaire will always be an intrusion into the life of the respondent, be it in terms of time taken to complete the questionnaire, the level of threat or sensitivity of the questions, or the possible invasion of privacy. (p 245)

However I was equally aware that a survey of this type would have limitations. A different style of questionnaire or an interview might well have elicited the deeper feelings and opinions the practitioners had about their setting's approaches to assessment. I was also acutely aware that participants might choose the answer they considered would be 'correct' rather than the one which truly reflected their practice. I tried to discourage this in my accompanying letter but it remains a weakness of this kind of method that such distortion of reporting is possible. I believe, however, that the questionnaire method worked well for this study. I had a total of 59 responses and achieved my aim of reaching a wide variety of setting types. It also opened up many more potential areas for future research.

In an accompanying letter I also mentioned confidentiality. I was very aware that privacy would be paramount. My position as a county adviser can be helpful in encouraging practitioners to become involved but it can also appear threatening because of my overview role of early childhood provision within the county. Practitioners may be suspicious of the survey's purpose or use. A clearly worded letter would need to be sent with the survey to ensure that all practitioners were clear that their responses would be wholly confidential. Cohen *et al.* (2000) identify the functions of a respondent's involvement, such as the importance of obtaining their informed consent, their right to withdrawal at any stage and the offering of guarantees such as confidentiality and non-traceability within the research.

Care must be taken when designing a questionnaire to phrase questions so as to ensure that the respondents can say what they want to *rather than promoting the researchers agenda*' (Cohen *et al.*, 2000 p 246). The researcher must make every effort to avoid bias and ensure reliability of data. Morrison (1996) suggested that methodological rigour is an ethical and not simply a technical matter. Accordingly, I trialled the questionnaire before sending it to settings, in order to establish whether it would make sense to the reader, whether it was likely to be completed and whether it would produce the data I wanted.

Using a postal survey questionnaire enabled me to target a wide variety of settings and to obtain a large sample. The survey questionnaire was sent out to one hundred settings identifying a cross-section of provision. The settings were selected from the register for private and voluntary provision members of the county partnership, as well as from the local education authority's school list. Fifty maintained schools and 50 private and voluntary settings were selected, by taking every fifth setting on the two lists to reach one hundred in total. My mailing list consequently reflected a wide range of settings in diverse areas and the random selection precluded any bias. I chose to select a 50% sample of schools, as I wanted also to explore whether school settings had a different approach to assessment than the private and voluntary settings, particularly in their access to training and in the influence of school Ofsted inspection criteria and

Baseline Assessment materials. The questionnaire was closed and structured to allow for patterns to be observed and comparisons to be made. Because of the fairly large sample in the study, a structured questionnaire provided a method for analysing the resulting data. The data need to be reduced by coding and the use of a coding frame. Although this turned out to be time consuming, it was invaluable in making it possible to analyse and make sense of the large amounts of data collected in answer to the research questions.

The influence of national assessment practices and policy for standardised testing

Assessment was a focus in educational debate and practice throughout the 1980s, a period described as '*the era of assessment-led educational reform*' (Hargreaves, 1998 p99). Hargreaves believed 'assessment, more than curriculum or pedagogy' had been 'the prime focal point for educational change.' (Hargreaves, 1998 p99)

The introduction of the National Curriculum in England and Wales in 1989 sharpened the focus on assessment at all levels and led to a hardening in the view of the role of assessment in education. There was a shift from the developing concern (at all levels) with profiling and personal records of achievement, to an emphasis on standardised testing of a kind that is expected to provide evidence of success – and therefore also failure – to all those who are regarded as the '*consumers of educational provision*' (Blenkin and Kelly, 1992).

> Whether this assessment is statutory or non-statutory, it is being pressed upon schools and teachers at all levels as the focal point of their professional concerns. (p2)

The impact of such assessment has been an accelerated move towards increased testing even where such testing is non-statutory.

Whether statutory or non-statutory, testing cannot be ignored and this is especially worrying in the light of the unsuitability of some public forms of assessment in the education of very young children. The main focus of educational policy throughout the 1990s has been externally prescribed and imposed testing. The first stage of this policy development was the work of the Task Group on Assessment and Testing (HMSO, 1988) which contained serious implications for all sectors, including early childhood settings in schools. The Rumbold report (1990) highlighted the pressure felt by early childhood practitioners to conform to these requirements.

> *Those working with the under fives have been concerned that there might be pressures upon them to respond inappropriately to the curricular requirements of the Education Reform Act. In particular, some have feared that there would be escapable pressure from parents and others to teach and test the formal skills of literacy and numeracy prematurely.* (Rumbold, 1990 pp128)

The significance of this for the early childhood curriculum has been the top-down effect of statutory testing at Key Stage one, and so the study reported here asked whether early childhood settings were resisting the 'pressure to respond inappropriately'?

With the exception of nursery schools, a small percentage of most of the setting types admitted to organising tests. Interestingly, 25% of private day care nurseries use organised tests and this was 5% higher than the next setting type, reception classes with 17%. What assumptions can we make from these findings? Are they due to parental expectation or to settings' interpretations of parent expectation? Some private day care nurseries are under pressure to work to a parental agenda because they are, effectively, paying customers. School based provision would argue that they, too, often bow to the pressure of parents' agendas. Parents are keen to know how their child is progressing. Many have spent time identifying the provision they thought best suited to the needs of their child and themselves. Parents may have established deep-rooted beliefs that testing indicates success or lack of it. Parents' perception of the value of formal testing may be influenced by the strong media attention directed to end of key stage testing and the use of this data to create school league tables.

> *Some parents, reading about low standards and the drive to raise outcomes in literacy and numeracy, think this represents 'education'. Parents must have access to information about the importance of a broad and balanced educational experience, and should be encouraged to make informed decisions about what experiences they want their children to have.* (The Early Years Curriculum Group, 2002 p5)

Parents' own experiences of schooling and testing may lead them to seek similar methods of indicating a high quality environment. Or maybe the setting itself is convincing parents of their value by endorsing the use of such methods? Rumbold argued that:

> Educators may themselves do much to avert such pressures by suitably involving and informing parents. (Rumbold, 1990 p128)

Fisher (2002) supported this view, suggesting that parents needed re-assurance that early education should be about providing deep and rich foundations rather than narrow and limiting outcomes.

What the survey questionnaire does not establish is what information the settings believed these tests produced, and how this is used to support children's learning. Blenkin and Kelly argued that:

> there is little evidence that any attempt has been made to acknowledge, let alone to act upon, the subtleties of the interrelationships between assessment procedures and curricular practices, and there is every indication that we are moving to a curriculum which is in every sense assessment-led or, worse, test-led. (Blenkin and Kelly, 1992 p3).

Consequently, assessment is not informing the curriculum that is offered to children or meeting their individual development needs. Bruce suggests that:

> If 'the best' is seen as only that which is measurable, that part of education which is offered to young children becomes narrower and narrower. (Bruce, 1987, p168).

The early years has traditionally been free of the constraints of public forms of assessment but this research study indicates that testing is now a method used in many early childhood settings to determine learning and teaching opportunities. As Blenkin and Kelly state:

> Current preoccupation with external testing is directed more at establishing means for controlling the curriculum than at raising the educational quality of what is offered to pupils in school. (Blenkin and Kelly, 1992 p3).

Can we therefore presume that the influence of testing within the early childhood setting is having a detrimental effect on the quality of the learning and teaching?

The influence of Baseline Assessment on practice

Other major initiatives introduced in 1996, some eight years after the Education Reform Act 1988, included proposals for the introduction of a *National Framework for Baseline Assessment* and the publication of the *Desirable Learning Outcomes for Children's Learning* (SCAA, 1996a, 1996b). All maintained primary schools in England had a statutory requirement from September 1998 to use an accredited Baseline Assessment scheme with all children starting in reception classes (or year 1 if this is when children first start school).

Schools were required (until September 2002) to assess a child in terms of: personal and social, language and literacy, and mathematical development within the first seven weeks after they were officially registered in a primary, infant, or special school, whether full or part-time.

As with the introduction of the SATs for primary schools, early years educators expressed great concern lest the statutory imposition of Baseline Assessment at five lead to an assessment-led curriculum in the early years '*with all the inherent dangers we witnessed at KS1*' (Blenkin and Kelly, 1992 p24). The survey questionnaire found that introduction of SATs had impacted on the early childhood setting as discussed earlier and suggested that the same was true in relation to Baseline Assessment.

Each setting type which replied to the survey used an informal baseline assessment. Of the settings surveyed, 27% carried out an informal baseline. Most notable was finding that five out of six nursery classes said that they use an informal baseline. This is probably not surprising in light of the increasing pressure on schools to show the 'value' they have 'added'. Schools use these methods of assessment to show the progress children make from the time they enter the school setting until they leave and for many schools this starts in the nursery class. They will also want to try where possible to standardise the assessment methods used in the Foundation Stage so, despite the introduction from September 2002 of the Foundation Stage Profile, informal application of the Baseline Assessment materials will continue to be a preferred choice for many schools.

It is worrying that 7% of the settings saying they use informal baseline come from the private and voluntary sector. We must question whether they actually have access to the Baseline Assessment schemes or whether they have interpreted the question to be about use of an assessment by which to indicate a child's starting point on entry. This also could equally apply to the nursery classes surveyed.

Another question would be the role parents play in a setting when identifying a child's starting point at entry to the setting. If baseline testing is promoted as the primary method of identifying a child's educational starting point, what value are we placing on the role of parents as a child's first educator? What value are these settings according the parents' wealth of expertise and the professional trust in using this information as a child's starting point indicator? Has the need for quantifiable data impacted so strongly that the beliefs of effective assessment processes in the early childhood setting are lost? Is the use of summative assessment rather than the rich and powerful use of formative data increasingly influencing the practice of early childhood settings? This study can only raise these important questions and suggest the need for further investigation.

What has happened to observation?

Observation has long been associated with effective assessment within the early childhood setting. As Nutbrown states

> To make effective and reliable assessments, teachers need to be open to what children are saying and doing, receptive to their ideas and respectful of their learning agendas. (Nutbrown, 1994 p 120)

Early years practitioners have always used observation to provide themselves with information about what children can and cannot do and used this information to plan for appropriate learning experiences to meet children's needs. It has always been considered the best and only way of establishing the complexity of a child's development (Bruce, 1987; Drummond et al., 1993; Hurst, 1997; Nutbrown, 1994). The information we have about Susan Issacs' school, the Malting House, is largely based on the detailed observation records she and her colleagues kept. The observations highlighted the differences between children, and the changes in their individual behaviour (1930). Assessment is not a new concept and is crucial to providing the best possible developmental opportunities for children. But how we carry it out, and the nature of its style and content, is crucial. Drummond and Pollard (1993) noted that:

> *Effective assessment is a process in which our understanding of children's learning, acquired through observation and reflection, can be used to evaluate and enrich the curriculum.* (p13)

Nutbrown (1999) was of the view that:

> *Through their work with children, teachers make judgements about children's ideas, what children know, their motivation, their abilities and their thinking and how their interests and ideas might further be developed. Such judgements are based upon what teachers in early education see children do and hear children say rather than formal assessments.* (p119)

She continues:

> *Regular and frequent observation is necessary if teachers are to build up a clear picture of individual children, the value of activities and group dynamics.* (p124)

High quality and frequent observation is at the heart of effective early childhood assessment but, given the influences of summative assessment, is this method of formative assessment practice still directly impacting on early childhood settings?

In this study 86% of the settings surveyed reported using informal observations (note taking at adult led learning activities and/or recording spontaneous moments). In contrast, less than half (only 44%) of settings surveyed used formal systematic observation in their current assessment practices (planned/focused observations such as child tracking or time sampling methods).

All the nursery schools surveyed used both methods, as did the six nursery classes. The picture for the other setting types, however, did not reflect this trend. Only 49% of reception classes, 42% of play groups and 38% of private day care nurseries said they used formal observation methods. The Rumbold Report highlighted the need for both types of observation:

> *The information gained from observing children's day-to-day activities may need to be supplemented by more focused observations of activities planned to show how well an individual or group of children is progressing.* (Rumbold Report, 1990 p126)

This was the first clear difference between types of provision revealed by the study. However this arises only between maintained school nursery provision and the other types of setting surveyed. Again the structure of the survey questionnaire does not allow us to draw firm conclusions regarding the possible reasons for this, but we can identify the following.

Firstly let's consider the position of school reception classes which has, in the past, been somewhat confusing. They have been under pressure to conform to the often inappropriate Key Stage one assessment requirements and these have recently tended more to formal methods such as testing and work-sampling. Hutchin warns against using work-sampling as the primary source of evidence when assessing children's achievements.

> It is neither a statutory requirement nor useful to keep samples of children's work at set points in time simply as proof of attainment. (Hutchin, 2000 p8)

Work-sampling was the most popular method of assessment in the based settings, used by 79% of reception classes and 67% of school nursery classes. Whereas the nursery classes surveyed reported using observation alongside work-sampling, only a small percentage of reception classes did so. What we can not determine from this study is the use of such samples and whether they are, as Hutchin suggests, used primarily to record attainment rather than to inform future development.

The survey suggests that observation is the least likely method of assessment to be seen in the reception class other than note-taking during adult directed activities. Since the introduction of the Foundation Stage, many practitioners are now faced with the task of re-skilling themselves in formal observation techniques. So it is not surprising that only 49% of reception classes surveyed use any form of formal observation.

The lack of advice and training may be the reason why the private and voluntary settings did not use formal observation. In 1999 Early Years Development and Childcare Partnerships were set up. Settings agreed to provide a quality curriculum and automatically became members of their county partnerships. Free training and advice was made available for all settings educating and caring for 4 and 5 year olds. For many settings this proved a challenging time, not least in the development of effective and manageable planning methods and the use of assessment to inform their planning. Partnership training and development plans for 2002-2003 are particularly concerned with the issue of planning and assessment but this is in its early stages and the continued expansion of assessment methods is likely to be addressed for some time to come. So it seems reasonable to suggest that some of the 41% of private and voluntary settings which are not using formal observation techniques in their practice are still improving their practice in other ways and may yet to develop their assessment methods.

The nursery provision surveyed carried out both informal and formal observations. Nursery provision has perhaps been less influenced by primary school assessment agendas so practitioners working within it have continued to implement their own practices throughout this time of change. Many of them have developed expertise in working with and assessing very young children and are likely to have received specialist training such as nursery nurse qualifications. This is unlikely to be available to the same extent to the private and voluntary sectors and the lack of early childhood education specialism in initial teacher training will certainly place practitioners trained in this way at a disadvantage.

Conclusions

This chapter has reported a study which indicates that the use of standardised testing in the primary phase of schooling and the introduction of Baseline Assessment has had an impact on all setting types in the maintained, private and voluntary sectors. Not only has it influenced the types of assessment methods they are using, but the use of good quality assessment methods long associated with effective early childhood practice, such as formal observations, are now carried out in only a minority of settings and primarily in maintained school nurseries.

From this study we can conclude that assessment is considered by all settings to be important and a great deal of time and effort is spent on collecting information about children's learning. What is worrying however, is whether the methods currently in use are appropriate and useful. To what extent will current assessment practices as revealed in this study provide information on which to base the planning of appropriate learning opportunities for each child's development? The study has illustrated that some current methods of assessment serve primarily as records of attainment and do little to support curriculum planning effectively. This is due primarily to the nature of the methods used. If the assessment tools used are not formative devices – including the involvement of parents or the use of formal systematic observation – then the wealth of a child's development opportunities may be ignored or inadequately met.

Early childhood practitioners must therefore remain focused on the ultimate aim of assessment:

> The primary purpose of assessment is to ensure that educational provision can be planned and evaluated appropriately to serve children's needs. (Rumbold Report, 1990 p 129)

References

Athey, C. (1990) *Extending Thought in Young Children*, London:Paul Chapman Publishing

Blenkin, G. M. and Kelly, A. V (Eds) (1992) *Assessment in Early Childhood Education*, London: Paul Chapman Publishing.

Bruce, T. (1987) *Early Childhood Education*, London: Hodder and Stoughton

Clark, S. (1998) *Targeting Assessment in the Primary Classroom*, London: Hodder and Stoughton

Cohen, L., Manion, L. and Morrison, K. (2000, fifth edition) *Research Methods in Education*, London: RoutledgeFalmer

Drummond, M. J and Nutbrown, C. (1992) 'Observing and assessing young children' in Pugh, G. (ed) *Contemporary Issues in the Early Years*, London: Paul Chapman Publishing in association with the National Children's Bureau.

Drummond, M. J. and Pollard, A. (1993) *Assessing Children's Learning*, London: David Fulton

Fisher, J. (Ed) (2002) *The Foundations of Learning*, Buckingham: Open University Press

Hargreaves, A. (1998) *Curriculum and Assessment Reform*, Buckingham: Open University Press

HMSO, (1988) *The 1988 Education Reform Act*, London.

Hurst, V. (1997) *Planning for Early Learning, Educating Young Children*, London: Paul Chapman Publishing

Hutchin, V. (2000) *Tracking Significant Achievement in the Early Years*, Second Edition, London: Hodder and Stoughton.

Issacs, S (1930) *Intellectual Growth in Young Children*, London:Routledge and Kegan Paul.

Mac Naughton, G., Rolfe, S. and Siraj-Blatchford, I. (2001) *Doing Early Childhood Research*, Buckingham: Open University Press.

Morrison, K. R. B. (1996) 'Why present school inspections are unethical', *Forum*, Vol. 38, no.3, p79-80.

Nutbrown, C. (1994) *Threads of Thinking: young children learning and the role of early education*, London:Paul Chapman Publishing

Rumbold Report (1990) *Starting with Quality*, London: HMSO.

SCAA. (1996a) *Baseline Assessment and Value Added*, Report to SCAA, London:DFEE

SCAA. (1996b) *Nursery Education: Desirable Outcomes for Children's Learning on Entering Compulsory Education*, London: DFEE Publications.

The Early Years Curriculum Group, (2002) *Onwards and Upwards, Building on the Foundation Stage* London: Early Years Curriculum Group.

Vygotsky, L.S. (1978) *Mind in Society*, Cambridge, Mass: .Harvard University Press,

Wilson, N. and Mclean, S. (1994) *Questionnaire Design: A Practical Introduction*, Co. Antrim: University of Ulster Press.

This chapter is dedicated to Moira Lauder

5

Children's assessment of their own learning

Debbie Critchley

Introduction

My study originated from an interest in Feuerstein's *Mediated Learning Experience* (MLE). It was stimulated by a recent study of the key aspects of Feuerstein's MLE (Howell, 1999) which suggested that tertiary students and their teachers had different views on the importance of one aspect of MLE: students assessing their own progress.

According to Howell's (1999) survey, students attached much greater importance than their teachers to this issue. My Teaching English as a Foreign Language (TEFL) experience suggested to me that if tertiary teachers, described by Howell as 'professional, experienced EFL teachers of adults', assigned low priority to students assessing their own learning, it would be less likely that teachers of younger students would attempt the process in their classrooms, given that younger EFL students generally require more organisation of their activities and are more teacher dependent than adult students. Older students can engage in activities with greater independence, while the teacher works with individuals or small groups. Issues of self-access and learner independence are therefore significant in this debate.

I carried out a small-scale exploratory study into students assessing their own progress with 4-5 year old primary children being taught in English, and with 10-14 year old elementary level EFL students.

Groups where problems were likely to arise because of their young age or elementary level of English were deliberately chosen with the aim of realistically assessing the classroom considerations of planning, time and classroom management. I also wanted to see how younger children would handle the concept of their own progress.

In this abridged version of the study I focus on the methods used with the younger children and the related findings, one of which concerns the differences between young children's perspectives on progress and those of older children and adults. I also discuss issues related to independent learning which enable the individual or small group work of self-assessment to take place.

Feuerstein's 'Mediated Learning Experience'

Fundamental to this study is Feuerstein's work and its potential (Feuerstein, Rand and Rynders, 1988). Williams and Burden (1997) describe twelve key features of the MLE which they have adapted to language learning and summarised thus:

- *significance*
- *purpose beyond the here and now*
- *shared intention*
- *a sense of competence*
- *control of own behaviour*
- *goal-setting*
- *challenge*
- *awareness of change*
- *a belief in positive outcomes*
- *sharing*
- *individuality*
- *a sense of belonging*

(Williams and Burden, 1997:69)

The mediator role could be considered an extension of the teacher's role and though many teachers would perhaps be content to achieve certain of these goals Feuerstein opines that the majority should be routinely attained.

This study refers largely to Williams and Burdens' adaptation (1997), rather than Feuerstein's original (1988), as their work provided the basis for the questionnaire employed by Howell (1999) in her survey.

Howell's findings

Howell conducted a survey of 181 students and 23 TEFL teachers in tertiary education in the Gulf, using Williams and Burdens' 1996 survey based on Feuerstein's MLE. The results indicated a marked difference between the importance attached by teachers to the issue of enabling students to assess their own progress, and by their adult students (Howell, 1999 p 9). Students ranked this issue sixth – at the midpoint – in importance, while teachers placed it twelfth or last.

Independent learning

Given that students' learning is individual, time has to be created for teachers to discuss progress with students when the other students in the class are actively engaged without needing teacher input. In tertiary education the classroom management involved is fairly simple. However, in EFL, with children and elementary level learners, realistic classroom management issues are rather more complex.

At the English-medium primary school where I carried out the study, each year group had an area where children participated in independent learning. Here, the teacher and helpers could work with individuals or small groups, perhaps on their reading or writing.

In large EFL institutes, with limited space and profit-making priorities, a resourced area is rarely available. Self-access centres are generally a recent addition to EFL institutes. For example, a large global institute I worked for added a self-access centre to a South American branch in the early 1990s and in Jordan and the Gulf, such centres were added in the late 1990s. Often, however, self-access centres are orientated towards adult learners.

Ideally, a year one language learning classroom will have its own self-access section which is in frequent use. Jackson (1998) suggests a corner comprising a worksheet bank, reader and reference library, listening station and stationery, with a computer and language orientated software. A reading scheme could provide a good start but, as Williams and Burden observed, 'It is important to note that learner autonomy involves more than the provision of suitable self-access materials' (1997 p68).

Nor does independence develop unaided. Many sources refer to the challenging nature of beginning a culture of learner independence. Here it is important to consider that students spend fewer hours in the EFL environment than in their schools and the two experiences may contrast greatly. In school, they may be expected to sit in rows in very large classes and wait until they are asked a question individually by the teacher. The strategies they use at school may therefore be very different from those required of them in the EFL classroom. Williams and Burden warn that:

> Young children will initially need more direction from their teachers and need to be helped gradually to take on more responsibility for their learning as they become more self-directed. (1997 p71)

Learner autonomy is sometimes interpreted as simply leaving students to do their own thing. In my work with Spanish, Latin American and Arab Students, I found that all of them have needed guidance in becoming autonomous. Investment of time in learner autonomy training therefore seems particularly worthwhile in contexts where the students have little prior concept of independent learning.

Also, learner autonomy does not necessarily refer to students working alone. Lee highlights that 'interaction, negotiation, collaboration etc., are important factors in promoting learner autonomy' (Lee, 1999 p283). Teachers might feel that it will be harder to encourage young learners than adults to be independent. However, it could be argued that the opposite is true, perhaps because of the flexibility of younger learners.

Polk Lillard (1997), writing about her experiences running a Montessori classroom, promotes the view that independence is essential and thus: 'it is apparent to me that independence is a necessity if the child's drive to develop is to be realised.' She adds the distressing but cautionary point that, 'However, in many of my five-year-olds the desire for independence has already been driven underground by discouraging adults or an alien environment' (1997 p4).

During the initial stages of building independence the work-load for teachers might seem heavier than usual. But there should be a payoff in the long-term.

All these issues applied to the 10-14 year old group with whom I carried out my study, and led to my choice of paper-based materials in the promotion of their self-awareness of progress. This allowed all students to complete surveys simultaneously, but individual discussion with students was not feasible. The students were studying for only two hours a day during a three-week summer course, so training opportunities were time-constrained. The students appeared to have a limited concept of independent learning and their behaviour required the teacher's constant attention. The 4-5 year olds, however, were already accustomed to independent learning and there was suitable scope to interview the students individually or in small groups.

Methods and methodology
Participatory research with children
Many sources discuss the role of the researcher in the eyes of the young participants (see, for example, Christensen and James, 2000). I acted as a parent helper with the reception class of 4-5 year olds for the academic year from September 1999 to June 2000, and had established rapport with the students before I began my research in May. My own children were in the school so the children also saw me after school, often taking time to chat and show me work they were taking home. At first I felt that some children were a little reticent about working with me. But by giving them individual attention and much positive feedback, I apparently overcame this reticence and the children appeared confident in my presence.

Christensen and James note a paradigm shift: whereas children in the past were the object of research, today's children are often the participants (2000 p3). There has been an increase in participatory research *with* children rather than observation *of* them.

Christensen and James suggest that special methods are not necessary for research with children (2000 pxi), meaning that children can take part in structured and unstructured interviews and complete questionnaires (2000 p2). The possibility of completing questionnaires clearly depends on the level of the child's literacy. In addition, interviews need to be extremely short and focused, partially because of some shorter attention spans but also because methods need to be familiar to the children and thus make 'human sense' to them, avoiding the criticism levelled at much of Piaget's work (Donaldson, 1987).

Interviewing children

The children interviewed were selected fairly arbitrarily from within the class, according to who was present on a given day and who was not busy reading with the teacher. I was careful to interview children with a range of language backgrounds: native speaker, bilingual and other home language. Eighteen children were interviewed altogether, some of them more than once. The first interview focused on their progress and the second on their reasons for learning. Some children were only available to be interviewed once on one topic only. The children's responses were highly illuminating.

Methodologically, the possibility of bias in interviews needs considering. Writing on the topic of solitary interviewers Gavron (1966) noted that: 'It is difficult to see how this [bias] can be avoided completely' but advised that 'awareness of the problem plus constant self-control can help'. I found the tape recorder a great help to my subsequent understanding of and sensitivity to differences of tone of voice and emphasis. Immediately after each interview we played back the recording for the interviewee's enjoyment. I could hear, to my dismay, unconscious changes in my own intonation which could have suggested to the children that I favoured answers related to the academic over those related to the social sphere. This provided further evidence of the need for great care to demonstrate equal interest in all types of responses. On further analysis of the tapes and transcripts, however, I found that the children appeared not to notice my shifts in intonation, or at least that none of them altered their answers as a result. The experience highlighted the advantage of tape recording over note-taking.

The interviews took the form of short spells of asking only two questions at a time, slotted into the work I usually did with the children. Holmes found the strategy of interviewing children while they were drawing successful (1998 p 23) but when I tried this the children were so busy drawing that they were not keen to talk! The interviews were flexibly structured in that two key questions were outlined, with flexibility in the wording of the questions, thus reflecting Vygotsky's

ZPD which states that carers reword the questions according to the understanding of their charges (Tharp and Gallimore, 1988).

The first interviews took place a week earlier than planned due to an unexpected opportunity in class when I was asked to review the children's work with them. The previous week I had reviewed work from two successive weeks with one of the students, comparing it noting his progress. I decided to try this approach with other students, reviewing their work from the previous term which was compiled in large workbooks.

I began by asking two students the open request to 'have a look through your books and see if you can find things you are now better at'. This technique did not focus the children's attention on progress as I had hoped. Instead they made general comments such as, 'Look, I didn't finish this!' or 'I like that drawing'. During this process I asked them to comment on what they had got better at and what they looked forward to getting better at 'in year one.' Their teachers were orientating the pupils to the concept of moving to a new class next year, stressing the positive aspects while giving the children time to work through their feelings about it. So the idea of looking forward to the next class was already familiar to the children.

I aimed to record the conversations on tape, as taking notes while participating in activities with children would result in gaps in the notes and interruptions in the activities. On this first occasion, however, no tape recorder was available so I took notes but missed a few of the children's remarks and was convinced that using a tape recorder was more appropriate for the main part of my study.

I was aware that I needed to be careful about the wording of questions. On interviewing students, Holmes advises, 'The key is to avoid misleading questions or getting the children to say what you want to hear' (1998 p 23). The tape recorder was again to prove useful here as playing each short segment back to the interviewees heightened my awareness. Holmes also suggests tailoring the questions to the children's language ability, which can vary greatly.

Ethics of involvement

The names of the children have been changed here to protect their identity but other information about them, including their gender, remains unchanged. Permission was obtained from the school and parents.

Despite current ethical thinking, I did not explain the research to the children before our interviews nor was any work done in class about what progress means, as I aimed to generate a view of children's own perspectives on their progress rather than providing them with adult perspectives. The phrase I used: 'get better at' was chosen because I thought it to be both understandable and relevant to children's everyday experience.

In addition to the interviews with the children I kept a journal of my work with them and what I was learning from it. The journal entries helped me to draw together the information I had about each child's strengths and the methodology of the study as a whole.

Findings and discussion

Asking such young students to look for signs of progress in their work raised some methodological issues. Particularly, there was too much for the children to focus on so they sometimes became distracted. One child compared two similar pieces of work and, because she saw progress in terms of visual data such as neatness of letter shape, perceived the neater work to be of better quality. In another instance where a child compared his two pieces of writing, he declared the earlier piece to be better. He said that the writing in his preferred piece looked neater, and it did. But, as I explained to him, the earlier work had been copied from a slip of paper, whereas he had written the latter independently and had clearly been concentrating more on the words and meaning than letter formation. That the independent effort did not represent progress in his eyes can be a problem for teachers, and they need to ensure that their views do not dominate children's opinions when they select work to represent children's progress.

Nikolov (1999 pp42-43) studied three groups of children aged 6-8, 8-11, and 11-14 and reported that utility reasons for learning EFL (such as 'to travel abroad') increased significantly with age and that 'classroom related reasons' such as 'because it's nice' were prominent among the younger age group. Nikolov also noted that a few 6-8 year olds gave teacher-related reasons such as 'because the teacher has long hair'. One of the children in my study noted that he learnt things at school 'because you say so' and when I asked him about things he learnt outside of school, he replied 'because my dad says so.'

My own findings supported Nikolov's, though I found a difference in concepts between the two different age groups, with the 10-14s closer to the adult focus. For example, when the younger children were asked why they were learning to do all these things many replied that they did so to progress to the next school year or into junior school or a new school. They did not seem to have personalised aims, whereas the older group all expressed – in writing in English or Arabic – what seemed more personalised aims, such as to attend an English speaking school, or to obtain a good job or for travel abroad. All fourteen of the students in the 10-14 group gave a utility reason, bar one who said 'Because I like writing and speaking in English'. I also found a difference in context: the reception children were attending compulsory schooling, the TEYL students studying in additional English classes.

Muschamp noted that 5-9 year olds in her study 'could all talk to varying degrees about the progress they had made' (1994 p 230). I would add that the 4 to 5 year olds I interviewed all spoke about their progress. But their ideas of what constituted progress differed from those of the adults. The following is an example of a typical conversation:

DC: What have you learnt this year that you're pleased about?
Danny: Drawing zebras
DC: Anything else?
Danny: Jumping rabbits
DC: Anything else that's not drawing?
Danny: Colouring clowns
DC: Is there anything you need to practise more?
Danny: [drawing] beds

Many of the children expressed their progress and future aims in terms of drawing. They did so independently as each one overheard only one other student and none appeared to have exchanged information about the questions they were asked. A second child taking part in the interview, for example, answered the first question, 'What have you learnt this year that you're pleased about?' by saying 'Doing work like adding' and to the question 'Is there anything you need to practise more?' he replied 'Take away'. Such responses relating to reading, writing or maths were untypical, whereas four out of six children on the first day of interviews noted that they had got better at drawing.

I was surprised by the frequency of references to drawing. The classroom teacher was also surprised, commenting that 'we don't do that much drawing' and suggesting that she would expect the children to view their progress in terms of the work focused on most in the classroom: initial reading, writing and numbers. The children's perspective suggested that for them progress in drawing was important and desirable – often forming part of their classroom and out of school experience and being also something they could see and feel – so progress was immediately visible.

Other children expressed their progress in terms of playground activity and swimming, though the latter was again clearly from a child's perspective – 'I can now open my eyes under water' – rather than an adults' perspective of distance achieved. Relating to the broader curriculum (Webber, 1999; Williams, 1998), a typical response was 'I'm better at library', referring to activities in the library such as choosing books, listening to a story and behaving appropriately. Danny, who talked earlier of his progress and who wanted to improve his drawing and colouring skills, was given his school report a week later. When asked what he thought it would say, he replied 'that I'm good at colouring'. In fact it recorded that he was good at reading, writing and science, and its format contained neither scope for a student's self-assessment nor any reference to artistic skills.

The mismatch here between the child's perspective and the adult perspective represented by the school report is stark. The fact that the child's view is neither elicited nor considered in many such situations could lead a child to abandon his or her view of progress and achievement in favour of the accepted, adult view of progress – and this would not be because of reaching mutual ground but because the child's view had gone unnoticed. This has implications for pupil's roles in assessment later in their school careers.

Feasibility and considerations of time, planning and classroom management

Whilst oral self-assessment is possible with young children, it is a time consuming process. Even working with only two children at a time, I found note-taking difficult. On replaying the tape of my interviews I found many comments I had initially missed due to the children both talking at once. Training for children in listening attentively, as described by Nunan and Lamb (1996), would possibly allow class discussion of progress to take place at circle-time. Classes with a common language could discuss progress in their first language, teacher's proficiency or availability of translator permitting.

The questionnaire format I used with the older children was more easily administered and took less time that the interviews with the younger children. Colleagues were keen to pilot the questionnaire with the 10-14 year olds, believing it would offer valuable insights in return for relatively little additional time and effort. As noted so succinctly by one of the teachers surveyed by Howell (1999), 'Time restricts practice.' Methods need to be sought which are practical and time efficient in addition to offering breadth.

What should be assessed and how are continually taxing questions. Some learning gains are difficult to assess, such as enjoyment of reading, and here personal targets, portfolios or profiles could provide a better means of identifying progress.

Self access and learner autonomy

The desirability of developing self-access materials, or acquiring such resources and developing the routines and attitudes needed to use them, can be promoted so as to free time for the teacher to work individually with students and encourage them to take responsibility for their own learning. Developing pupils' learning or metacognitive skills to do this can be advantageous. As Hedge notes, 'It is with students who have learnt passivity from their previous educational experience that we may see most value in learner training' (2000 p100).

Reviews and target-setting

Children develop at different rates and it appears that learning is non-linear, as argued by Munn (1996 p20-21) – and demonstrated in this study. Consequently, goals set for a whole class may be inappropriate for some of the individuals. Developing short-term individual achievable goals for students to work towards is more likely to be beneficial. Such goals should be negotiated with each student, as involving students in their own assessment has many advantages.

My study was exploratory. The work with the reception class took place towards the end of the academic year. For these reasons and due to time constraints in the TEYL class, the processes of target-setting and reviewing were not included. However, for self-assessment to be on-going and valuable to the learning process, these two elements are needed. For teachers and students to meet individually to negotiate and review short-term targets, teachers need to be relieved from timetabled class teaching.

Implications for further study

Further trial of Feuerstein's work in the language classroom could prove valuable, as little critical analysis is available yet. Feuerstein's view of what is needed for learning to take place could also be compared with those of other writers.

Study into children's perceptions of what they are good at and how much this depends on the expressed opinions of significant others could also add fascinating insight into this field.

Visual material such as a book or wall display of the progress of a whole class, with individual work later added to each child's portfolio, could be produced as an extension of this study.

Reflexivity could be encouraged in children by giving them a larger part to play in the research process, such as designing and carrying out the research. This could address many of the issues of learner autonomy, responsibility and self-direction while children understand what progress can mean. Further study into methods of relating target-setting and reviewing to the self-assessment process could also be valuable.

Whatever we do it is clear that we must be careful truly to listen to children (Roberts, 2000).

References

Christensen, P. and James, A. (eds.) (2000) *Research with Children: perspectives and practices* London: Falmer Press

Donaldson, M. ((2nd edition 1987) *Children's Minds* London: Collins Fontana

Feuerstein, R. Rand, Y. and Rynders, J. (1988) *Don't accept me as I am: helping 'retarded people to excel'* New York: Plenum Press

Gavron, H. (1966) *The Captive Wife* London: Routledge and Keegan Paul

Hedge, T. (2000) *Teaching and Learning in the Language Classroom* Oxford: Oxford University Press

Holmes, R. (1998) *Fieldwork with Children* London: Sage

Howell, E. (1999) 'The Significance of Aspects of Feuerstein's Mediated Learning Experience to English Language Teachers and Students in the Higher Diploma Program of the Higher Colleges of Technology', unpublished paper for the Ed. D course at Exeter University

Jackson, A (1998) 'Learner Independence in the Primary School', *IATEFL Newsletter*, Issue No. 142, April-May p 11-12

Lee, I. (1998) 'Supporting greater autonomy in language learning' *ELT Journal* Vol. 52/4 October

Munn, P. (1996) 'Progression in Learning Literacy and Numeracy in the Preschool' in Hughes, M. (ed.) *Progression in Learning* Clevedon: Multilingual Matters Ltd. pp15-23

Muschamp, Y. (1994) 'Target setting with young children' in Pollard, A and Bourne, J. *Teaching and Learning in the Primary School,* London: Routledge

Nikolov, M. (1999) 'Why do you learn English?' 'Because the teacher is short'. A study of Hungarian children's foreign language learning motivation' *Language Teaching Research*, 3,1 pp33-56

Nunan, D. and Lamb, C. (1996) *The Self-directed Teacher: managing the learning process,* Cambridge: Cambridge University Press

Polk Lillard, P. (1997) *Montessori in the Classroom,* New York, Schocken (Previously published as Polk Lillard, P (1980) *Children Learning* New York: Schocken)

Roberts, H. (2000) 'Listening to Children: and Hearing them' in Christensen, P and James, A. (eds) (2000) *Research with Children: Perspectives and Practices* London: Falmer Press p225-240

Tharp, R. and Gallimore R. (1988) *Rousing minds to life: teaching, learning and schooling in social context,* New York: Cambridge University Press

Webber, B (1999) 'Assessment and Learning' in David, T. (ed.) (1999) *Teaching Young Children* London: Paul Chapman Publishing p 139-150

Williams, M. (1998) 'Ten principles for Teaching English to Young Learners' *IATEFL Newsletter* Issue No.142, April- May 1998, p 6-7

Williams, M. and Burden, R. (1997) *Psychology for Language Teachers: a Social Constructivist Approach* Cambridge: Cambridge University Press

A version of this chapter was first published in Clough, P. and Nutbrown C. (eds) (2001) *Voices of Arabia: Essays in Educational Research* Sheffield: University of Sheffield, School of Education

6

A 'Box full of feelings': developing emotional intelligence in a nursery community

Polly Dyer

To be emotionally literate is to be able to handle emotions in a way that improves your personal power and improves the quality of life around you. Emotional Literacy improves relationships, creates loving possibilities between people, makes cooperative work possible, and facilitates the feeling of community. (Steiner and Perry, 1997 p11)

Introduction

The *Box Full of Feelings* in the title of this chapter could describe our nursery, particularly on a wet day when tempers are high. It actually refers to an eponymous kit inspired by Professor Ferre Laevers (University of Belgium) and developed by Julia Moons and Marina Kog with the Centre for Experiential Education (EXE). Like the Effective Early Learning project based at the University of Worcester and latterly Birmingham University in the UK, EXE is concerned with the quality of education offered to young (nursery and primary) children and regards children's levels of *involvement* and *well-being* as a more valid measure of that quality than is perhaps possible with Baseline Assessments or SATS tests for example as currently used in the UK. The Box's manual explains:

Children are involved in their activities when they are deeply engaged in them, displaying energy and concentration. Children who show involved activity are 'at their best'. They feel challenged and are functioning near their full potential... Children who feel they are worthless, who lack the courage to undertake things, or who are emotionally tense, hardly ever or maybe never become involved in an activity. In other words, 'feeling good' is an essential condition for becoming involved in an activity. (Moons and Kog, 1997 p7)

This chapter describes a piece of ethnographic research which I carried out as a participant observer to explore ways of developing emotional intelligence. I am a nursery teacher in two part-time state nursery classes in an average sized primary school in southern England. Using the Box Full of Feelings, we focused specifically on helping children to recognise certain emotions – anger, sadness, happiness, fear – in themselves and others and, by developing ideas already in use in the nursery, we sought to increase children's sense of well-being, agency and ability to involve themselves in the social curriculum and thus make better use of it generally. As a staff we aimed to help the children but there were possibilities for growth for parents and staff too.

Defining Emotional Literacy

To be emotionally literate is to be able to handle emotions in a way that improves your personal power and improves the quality of life around you. Emotional Literacy improves relationships, creates loving possibilities between people, makes cooperative work possible, and facilitates the feeling of community. (Steiner and Perry, 1997, p11)

Part of being emotionally intelligent is having a well developed sense of morality and personal integrity. As Aristotle wrote in *The Nicomachean Ethics*:

Anyone can become angry – that is easy. But to be angry with the right person, to the right degree, at the right time, for the right purpose, and in the right way – that is not easy.

There has been growing concern world wide about the damage caused to societies and individuals by people's lack of emotional intelligence (Robertson, 1999; Goleman, 1996). Others write about the complex challenges that face children growing up in the twenty first century (Claxton, 1999; Abbott and Ryan, 1999). There is concern even within Government that its utilitarian preoccupation with raising literacy and numeracy standards is distorting traditional early childhood educational values ('Post' Report, June 2000). Studies of children's neurobiological development (see Gopnik, Meltzoff and Kuhl, 1999) and of 3-5 year olds' social understanding (see Gussin

Paley, 1986, 1992) indicate that there is cause for concern about the development of children's emotional well-being.

The purpose of the research was not so much to mould useful future citizens as to empower individuals. The project focused on the children, but it quickly became evident that it should also include the emotional and ethical quality of relationships between children and staff, staff and parents, and among the staff. The research focus also made it easier to discuss curriculum values, aims and innovations, as we became clearer about ethical and emotional implications. As an example, Gussin Paley in *You Can't Say You Can't Play* (1992) argues that it is unfair and morally untenable to expect children to deal unaided with social rejection and its consequences; that adults have a responsibility to change the order of things, however long it has been accepted as natural. It took much careful preparation and many illustrative and exploratory stories, but when we officially established the rule, '*You Can't Say You Can't Play*' the children were not only supportive but also relieved.

Methodology: tools for ethnography

Research is always a statement of a personal world view. (Clough, 2001)

The work discussed in this chapter was stimulated by the nationally established, action research-based Effective Early Learning project (Pascal and Bertram, 1997). In our school this work involved the Nursery, Reception and Year 1 classes and the role of the nursery in Effective Early Learning (EEL) was acknowledged to be successful. But I still felt concerned about the children's levels of well-being and whether all children (and possibly parents) really felt included in the nursery and able to make full use of all opportunities to learn.

I kept a journal, a 'slice of life' in the nursery, which became my field notes and the main record of the way the research into developing emotional intelligence progressed. This journal stands as a running commentary of thoughts; reflections on the relevant literature; on the observations I was also recording of children's actions, conversations, thoughts, perceived or explained feelings; and of the thoughts and comments that arose in conversations with staff and parents in the course of the research. In addition, there were interviews with colleagues and extended e-mail conversations about aspects of emotional intelligence and its implementation. I sent out a questionnaire to find out more about what children thought of the two toy bears who played an important role in the research, and some similarly placed puppets. The bears' journals, written and illustrated by the children and their parents, provided evidence of the variety of ways in which each family used its emotional intelligence to tell their story of a bear's visit to their home. A number of sources generated a large quantity of data, not all of which feature in the discussion in this chapter – such is the nature of ethnography.

I do not intend to discuss in detail the methodological arguments needed to make the case properly for my use of ethnography, but the following account will give a brief outline of my reasoning.

Action research was the right methodological approach for the EEL project; its democratic values of full participation of practitioners coincided with our own, as did its traditionally ethical purpose (Reason and Bradbury, 2001) to effect improvement within the institution by a continuous cycle of systematic evaluation, analysis, hypothesis, action and re-evaluation. However, there were two main problems with using action research to investigate this particular issue. Firstly, the sensitive nature of research into emotional intelligence, such as relationships with colleagues, children and parents, means it can only work where there is a strong, cohesive, highly motivated team. We were not yet at that stage. Secondly, action research 'tests' practice, but this research issue needed to be explored and its ramifications better understood before it could be handled so systematically – before it could be put to the test.

To present the research as a 'case' study would have involved me in similar difficulties: this was not an investigation, however illuminating it proved to be, into topics such as micro politics and patterns of influence. It needed to be an open ended exploration – in a sense, a 'felt' story woven out of my observations as I constructed the possible meanings and implications of what we were all learning. Ethnographic methodology proposes that the researcher is the 'research tool' (Pring, 2000; Pahl, 1999; Pollard, 1996). As Woods points out, ethnographers:

> are not trying to write fiction, of course – that is where the science comes in, in validating procedures and analysis. However in seeking to represent cultural

forms as they are lived by their owners, they have a common purpose with some novelists. How these are identified, comprehended and processed is more a matter of style, perception, interpretative processes, 'feel', sensitivities, an ability that is difficult to pin down but that involves empathising with others, an ability to 'understand' – essentially artistic properties – than a product of scientific method. (Woods, 1986, p6)

This was precisely what I needed; the ethnographic approach provided the flexible, open-ended 'medium' to carry my research 'message'.

Questions of generalisability, subjectivity and validity were all interrelated. For example, ethnographers recognise that subjectivity is both necessary and inescapable but acknowledging this allows researchers to use that subjectivity to help address issues of validity and generalisability in the process. Their work

> *... is based on the premise that social reality cannot be understood except through the rules which structure the relations between members of the group and which make it possible to interpret the actions, gestures and words of the others.* (Pring, 2000, p104)

And as Denzin writes:

> *Ethnographers can only produce messy texts that have some degree of verisimilitude; that is, texts that allow the readers to imaginatively feel their way into the experiences that are being described by the author.* (1997, p12)

So the truth of an account – the extent to which it is recognisable and so corroborated and useful to others – must also indicate how generalisable it is.

To give another example of a practical way to check material: when parents talked about their children, I immediately took notes in a way that would invite them to check my account. I would say things like: 'Have I got that right?' 'Is that what you meant?', 'That reminds me of the time he did....' And there would follow a discussion implicitly based on the agreed 'truth' of my opening observation.

Choosing to research emotional intelligence meant there were many ethical issues to consider: again I give two examples. First I was challenged by fellow research colleagues to think about whether it might be *un*ethical to teach children about their emotions; had I the right to do this to them? Could I deal with possible repercussions? Everything I had researched about the importance of emotional intelligence made it, I believed, unethical *not* to attempt it; the ethical concerns centred then round the *moral quality* of the teaching – the morality embedded within each teaching interaction. Suppose the 'pursuit of truth' conflicted with another research principle, the 'respect for the dignity and confidentiality' of the people in the study (see Pring, 2000, p143) as it would if an adult behaved badly towards a child – this would be an important piece of evidence in *this* research context, so I would preserve the emotional truth of the incident, but by telling a parallel narrative which would protect the identity of the person concerned. My argument is that the need to address how adults behave towards children outweighs the need to respect their possible wish to go unrecorded. (I was of course free to use examples of my own bad behaviour!)

Children's moral awareness: some findings

The material generated by the research was considerable and fell into four main areas:

- the need for emotionally intelligent adults
- the importance of friendship and play
- storytelling and emotional intelligence
- children's moral awareness.

The rest of this chapter focuses on children's moral awareness. This includes children's developing emotional intelligence: their moral courage, kindliness and generosity; their often sophisticated under-standing of their own and others' feelings and their need to feel good about themselves.

Children and adults need to learn together about emotional intel-ligence. Children are not passive recipients – they have much to teach adults – and their attitudes to each other continually challenge adults to reassess their own views. Matthews (1994) and Nutbrown (1996) both write about how taking the perspectives of children into serious account might radically alter our accepted values and codes of behaviour.

Sophie's treatment of the other children was something we all wrestled with, but it also illustrates all the points above and the necessity for dialogue – children with children, and children with adults – as we work through things together, not always getting it right, but needing to trust people's good intentions. The following extracts are taken from my research journal:

> Reading *The Moral Intelligence of Children* (Coles, 1997) – was struck again by Kizzie's observation that Sophie was angry (hitting people) ' cos they wouldn't be her friend, so be her friend and she won't hit you. She doesn't hit me.' Later (month later) Sophie bit her hard. Too much, Kizzie distressed, rejecting Sophie (as Sophie had her in a way). My solution later (after Sophie had resumed hitting) was to address the whole group again – we all love her but this hitting has to stop. All started saying what she'd done to them, I dismayed, not what I'd intended, Sophie didn't want to listen. Her mum said Sophie wouldn't hit unless other children were being mean to her, and Sophie had been worried all over the w/e about Kizzie, and hadn't wanted to come to school, was scared.

> We have to let this play out, don't we? Sophie needs that re-action, absolute moral rules – you *break* faith, people *lose* faith. But Coles (*ibid*, p195) reiterates what I understood before, simply 'be kind', rather than thinking in terms of what's the best thing to do. Coles says he pushed for answers, as 'a worried, literal-minded father, teacher'. But what he got was 'I told you... you have to be kind, that's what we have to be, to *do*: show by how we behave that we're interested in others and want the best for them.' And isn't that what Kizzie wanted for Sophie? Isn't it a question of our keeping faith with Sophie?

> Sophie pinched May and Bella because 'dey darfed at me when I dell over.' I was saying it was worse to pinch, but is it (colleague W) asked? She's right.

> Sophie knocked down Susie and Destiny's brick house. Both cross with her. Destiny came to me to complain. We talked to Sophie – 'are people allowed to knock down other's models?' Uncomfortable. She came to say sorry and kissed Susie. Susie won over, pretended to fall over with goofy look, Sophie delighted, Susie kissed *her*. Sophie now the centre, both Destiny and Susie saying – 'you *can* come in our house, you can come

in our car'. Very friendly, inviting, welcoming. Sophie en-
tranced.

Sophie walking round nursery all morning with Tom bear in her
arms, tender, solicitous, making sure he has the right clothes,
asking me to help her put them on, full of love for Tom. Every
now and then came to say, with conscious expression, as she bit
him or hit him on the head, 'I diting Tom bear/I durting 'im.' And
I would say, 'but he knows you love him?' and she'd smile and
hug him tightly.

Sophie stood up on the mermaid chair (a place to make
announcements) red splodge painting held up – and announced
'It's de dursery. It's Happy!' (What a testimonial!) Everyone
clapped.

It was clear to me that children needed to feel good about themselves, not only in the sense of knowing they were capable of great
bravery, or that they could take care of another child ('Josh: 'Give
me Aran' (a new child) '*I'll* look after him, I'll take care of him.') but
in the sense of being found lovable, no matter what, and this was
something that children sometimes seemed to have little control
over. This extract from my research journal illustrates the point:

I was talking with Ruby and she suddenly said, with an em-
barrassed smile, 'I hate myself.' I was shocked and asked her
why? She thought and said 'When I'm naughty.' I said I didn't
like myself when I'd done something I was ashamed about, but
if I tried to make things better, I didn't feel so bad. She nodded
but still looked unhappy. At storytime, I told a story about Faerybelle (I use these little puppet characters to tell stories about
classroom situations) who was horribly mean to poor Squeak
and, when reproached by the others, felt so bad that she went
away and hid in a corner, saying 'I hate myself.' Ruby, sitting
next to me, said delightedly, 'that's me!' and moved onto my
knee. Squeak and the others coaxed Faerybelle out of hiding,
and when I asked the children what the puppets should do to
make Faerybelle feel better, they all said, 'give her a hug'. Ruby
got one too.

Learning to be emotionally intelligent:
reaching conclusions

This final section briefly summarises the many conclusions to be drawn from this study.

Learning to be emotionally intelligent is a life-long process, and cannot be done in social isolation: parents, staff and children learn most effectively when they learn from each other in relationships characterised by openness, trust and warmth. Children have much to teach adults about morality, generosity, intuitive kindness, moral courage and an ability to play with emotional ideas in a way that adults may find harder to access.

All learning is complex, interactive and social: one's state of mind and individual character – whether child or adult – affects *what* one learns. Specifically: children showed higher levels of well-being, using criteria developed as part of the Box Full of Feelings kit, and were more involved, possibly as a result of the closer relationships between parents and staff, brought about by the nature of my research and its ongoing dialogue.

As a practitioner researcher the personal and professional rewards are considerable, but the discipline and critical reflection required also benefited the children and ensured real parental involvement. Furthermore, it is important for educational research in general that practising teachers are more fully involved. Carr (1995) writes:

> ...educational practice is morally committed action; it is an essentially ethical activity guided by basic educational values rather than narrow instrumental or utilitarian concerns. But although educational practice always involves moral purposes and intentions, these are construed not as 'ends' to which practice is the technical means, but as educational commitments that can only be realised in and through practice. (ibid, p49)

It is not simply that teachers can contribute an insider's perspective but also, as Carr cogently argues, a dialectical alliance between theorists and practitioners can help safeguard, even reinstate, educational aims and values, to better meet the concerns addressed in this chapter as they affect all our children.

References

Abbott, L. and Ryan, T. (1999) Learning to Go with the Grain of the Brain. *Education Canada,* Spring, 1999. (21st Century Learning Initiative: http://www.21learn.org)

Aristotle, The Nicomachean Ethics., in Goleman, D. (1996) *Emotional Intelligence: why it can matter more than IQ.* London: Bloomsbury

Carr, W. (1995) *For Education: towards a critical educational inquiry.* Buckingham: Open University Press

Claxton, G. (1999) *Wise Up: the challenge of lifelong learning.* London: Bloomsbury

Clough, P. (2001) Research and the construction of social policy Lecture, Sheffield: University of Sheffield, School of Education

Coles, R. (1997) *The Moral Intelligence of Children.* London: Bloomsbury

Denzin, N. (1997) *Interpretive Ethnography: Ethnographic Practices for the 21st Century.* Thousand Oaks, California: Sage Publications

Goleman, D. (1996) *Emotional Intelligence: why it can matter more than IQ.* London: Bloomsbury

Gopnik, A., Meltzoff, A. and Kuhl, P. (1999) *How Babies Think: the science of childhood.* London: Weidenfeld & Nicolson

Matthews, G. (1994) *The Philosophy of Childhood.* Cambridge, Mass.: Harvard University Press

Moons, J. and Kog, M. (1997) *A Box Full of Feelings* (manual) Centre for Experiential Education: University of Leuven

Nutbrown, C. (ed.) (1996) *Respectful Educators – Capable Learners: Children's Rights and Early Education.* London: Paul Chapman Publishing

Pahl, K. (1999) *Transformations: meaning making in nursery education.* Stoke-on-Trent: Trentham Books

Paley, V. G. (1986) *Mollie is Three: growing up in school.* Chicago: University of Chicago Press

Paley, V. G. (1992) *You Can't Say You Can't Play.* Cambridge Mass.: Harvard University Press

Pascal, C. and Bertram, T. (1997) *Effective Early Learning: case studies in improvement.* London: Hodder and Stoughton

Pollard, A. with Filer, A. (1996) *The Social World of Children's Learning: case studies of pupils from four to seven.* London: Cassell

Post Report (June 2000) *House of Commons Education and Employment Select Committee: Inquiry into Early Years Education.* London: The Parliamentary Office of Science and Technology

Pring, R. (2000) *Philosophy of Educational Research.* London: Continuum

Reason, P. and Bradbury, H. (eds.) (2001) *Handbook of Action Research: participative inquiry and practice* London: Sage

Robertson, I. (1999) *Mind Sculpture: unleashing your brain's potential.* London: Bantam Press

Steiner, C. with Perry, P. (1997) *Achieving Emotional Literacy: a personal program to increase your emotional intelligence.* London: Bloomsbury

Woods, P. (1986) *Inside Schools: ethnography in educational research.* London: Routledge

7

Working with families on curriculum: developing shared understandings of children's mark making

Christine Parker

It's about making his mark in the world. (a parent)

This chapter reports the development of a parents' focus group in a local education authority nursery school in the East Midlands, UK. The group investigated children's mark making and the opportunities for children to write, draw and make other kinds of marks at home.

The starting point for the study was the need to develop effective strategies for enhancing practitioner's partnership with parents and to establish a working model for enhancing parental involvement in the school.

The research questions
Consideration of the national context inspired three research questions:

1. *How can a nursery school involve parents in their children's mark making?*

Parental involvement in children's learning can benefit the learning and self-esteem of both children and adults (QCA, 2000; Whalley *et al.*, 2000) and strong links between mark making, talk and literacy offer the opportunity to discuss curriculum aspects that concern parents (Nutbrown and Hannon, 1997).

2. *What will participants learn about their children and children's mark making?*

The term participant includes everyone who is involved: parents, me, the school governor and the children. The more adults know and understand about children's theories, as represented through mark making, the more they are able to encourage and support children's learning (Rinaldi, 1997; Parker, 2001; Athey, 1990; Nutbrown, 1999a). The more adults become enthused by what they observe, the more confident they are to provide for the children's future development.

3. *What processes do the participants find useful about the shared experience?*

An aim of the study was that adult participants should be able to identify those processes that have been useful and those that are less successful. This could be shared with colleagues at school to implement a programme of regular parents' focus groups.

Parent and practitioner partnerships
The Foundation Stage
September 2000 saw the introduction of the Foundation Stage Curriculum in England and Wales (QCA, 2000). The Curriculum Guidance for the Foundation Stage promoted the development of positive partnerships with parents (QCA, 2000) but although there is an emphasis on working in partnership with parents, the scope is limited. In the description of how principles can be put into practice, the sharing of information on all aspects of the children's learning is clearly stated (QCA, 2000). Although the benefits of exchanging information with parents are discussed, how this can be achieved and the impact on children's learning is not emphasised.

How can we develop positive and effective partnerships?
The importance of developing parent-practitioner partnerships has been established through research over some decades in the United Kingdom (Rennie, 1996; Hannon and Nutbrown, 2001; Athey, 1990; Tizard and Hughes, 1981). The Froebel Early Education project (Athey, 1990) was successful in terms of developing parents' self-esteem and confidence and enhanced the parents' engagement in

their children's learning. The equality of opportunity given to each parent to participate in the project was significant, as was the parents' equal share in the discoveries encountered. The parents were recognised as participants in developing pedagogy and Athey suggests that this could be a model for replication (1990).

Work with parents at the Pen Green Centre in Corby, UK is influenced by Athey's research, being a study of 'involvement, well-being, adult style and schemas' (Arnold, 2001) whereby practitioners develop a practical approach to implementing parents' groups that is grounded in theory (Whalley *et al.*, 2001). In parallel, the *Raising Early Achievement in Literacy* (REAL) Project at the University of Sheffield (Nutbrown and Hannon, 1997) offers guidance on working with parents on aspects of early literacy. This chapter describes and discusses my action research as a pilot project for the future and draws on the considerable body of research into partnership with parents.

Common to all these projects is the understanding that parents want to be more involved and are excited by the opportunities that they present (Whalley *et al.*, 2001; Weinberger, 1997; Athey, 1990). Nutbrown (1999b) highlights the requirement to find out what parents want from their involvement. The projects have other factors in common such as: the children being the primary beneficiaries; respect for all participants; opportunities for open and trusting dialogue; and a grounding in educational philosophies of partnership based on articulated theories of learning. The development of shared language and understandings is at the forefront of partnership initiatives and this theme informs the consideration of research methodology later in the chapter.

Methodological and ethical research issues
The action research process
The action research process presents a researcher with an opportunity to focus in greater depth on an aspect of their field, in the hope that improvement or at least a clarification of the way forward for future development will result.

Identifying a problem

The focus for this action research study arose from a combination of events and concerns which place the study in a contemporary and political context:

- the Foundation Stage guidance (QCA, 2000) which acknowledges the value of parent and practitioner partnerships

- interest in the Reggio Emilia preschools and their ways of working with families (Malaguzzi, 1998)

- projects designed to involve parents (Nutbrown and Hannon, 1997; Whalley *et al.*, 2001)

Planning and implementation

Planning intervention requires time to consider ethical issues relating to entry into the research setting, requesting participant consent and ensuring participants are the primary beneficiaries of the research (Marsh, 2000). It is reassuring to remember that plans can be changed, as a response to needs identified in the research field. The dynamic nature of action research becomes apparent in the implementation of the programme. Graue and Walsh (1998) place great emphasis on the creative and active aspects of the research process, as do Dahlberg, Moss and Pence (1999). Abbott (1997) argues that the implementation of a variety of methods ensures a 'rich interpretation'.

Evaluation

I see the outcomes of this study as a beginning, not an end. This action research study is the beginning of future discourse between practitioners and parents (Dahlberg, Moss and Pence, 1999). Graue and Walsh (1998) emphasise the social nature of research: the researcher requires an audience and research does not occur in isolation and there is a hope that others will benefit. Abbott (1997) argues for research which focuses on specific aspects of the generated data rather than attempting to report on everything.

A consideration of ethical issues

Planning my study involved considering the validity of the project and negotiation with participants. Marsh (2000) presents a useful framework to enable researchers to consider ethical issues. Considering each process of the research allows the ethical issues that may arise to be identified. I adapted Marsh's framework by applying the action research study stages.

Themes relevant to all the processes in Table 1 relate to the researcher's personal ethics and attitudes: honesty, validity, originality, reliability, respect and open-mindedness.

Focus group and focused conversation

Within the context of this action research study, a focus group is defined as a group of adults who have a common interest, in the well-being of young children and their learning (Cohen, Manion and Morrison, 2000). Nutbrown (2002) argues for the use of focused conversations in terms of their dynamic and flexible nature. It is this aspect that adds vitality to my research study. Nutbrown's account of a focus group provides a useful model in terms of what it can feel like to participate (Clough and Nutbrown, 2002). Focus groups allow the research participants ownership of the project. The researcher has to follow the participants' thinking as opposed to having pre-determined outcomes, a position taken from the feminist research paradigm which considers 'researcher' and 'researched' to be equal participants (Clough and Nutbrown, 2002).

Nutbrown discusses the differences between focused conversation work and focus group interviews (Clough and Nutbrown, 2002): focus group interviews do not involve participants past the data generation stage. My perception is that our focus group is not initiated purely for research purposes but is a part of a bigger picture of school development. The purpose of the focus group does not stop with data generation; its participants are involved in focus conversation work as opposed to focus group interviews.

Ethical issues emerge in terms of power positions (Clough and Nutbrown, 2002). As the convenor of the group, it is inevitable that the participants will perceive me as the one with the knowledge and understanding. I do have a role in setting up the group and stating its purposes but it is important that the group moves towards shared ownership among everyone involved.

Table One: Ethical Consideration for the Study *Adapted from Marsh, (2000).*

Processes	Ethical Issues	Action to be Taken
Identifying a problem	Validity Originality Honesty Constructions of childhood Involvement of colleagues, respecting a range of opinions and ideas	Literature review to ensure relevant knowledge and understanding Reference to a code of ethics Participation in training Time for reflection and to question assumptions Self moderation Seek support from a critical friend
Planning an intervention	Reliability and validity Honesty Awareness of participatory research issues Understanding the setting and the needs of the participant	Review of literature concerning methodology Communication to all involved in the proposed study
Implementing an intervention	Participatory research issues: honesty, respect Data generation issues: Validity Accuracy Relevance Quality Consent to filling in a questionnaire the primary beneficiaries	Negotiation with all participants Non-involvement is an option Presentation of ideas to participants is clear and appropriate Monitor data as it is generated Involvement of participants in data generation ensures a range of perspectives Being reflective and reflexive, responding to the needs and suggestions of others The children and parents are the primary beneficiaries of the research process
Evaluating the outcome	Honesty Quality of reporting: Clarity and relevance Plagiarism Originality Awareness of the public arena Confidentiality	Having critical friends, request others to check validity. Proof reader Participant involvement Awareness of academic requirements Use of pseudonyms. Continue to consult with participants, children and adults to ensure continuing consent.

The action research
The parents' focus group

The aim of the study was to establish a working model for parental involvement in a nursery school, to investigate the potential of a parents' focus group and evaluate the effectiveness of processes. I wanted to provide parents with the opportunity to meet in an atmosphere of mutual respect where they felt comfortable and confident to contribute to the conversations. As a focus I chose an aspect of children's learning which would have immediate interest for parents: children's mark making.

Forming the group

My aim was to convene a group of six parents to discuss children's mark making. I took a personal approach, speaking individually to parents who had shown an interest in the school's activities. I invited parents who had previously worked in the school and who I thought would have time to participate fully. Eight families were involved, with a total of five girls and three boys aged 3:9-4:4 years. Three of the children had no siblings, one had one and four children had two siblings each. This method of selection is a weakness in the study: the issues of how to involve 'hard to reach' parents or parents who would need childcare or those who would prefer to attend out of session time have not been addressed here (see Arnold, 2001). When I approached selected parents personally, their responses were positive. I must also acknowledge that though I talk of 'parents' they were all mothers. Another issue for future work.

The meetings

Seven meetings were held on consecutive Friday mornings. The mothers' attendance varied: one attended one meeting, one attended two and another three meetings. Three parents attended six meetings and two all seven.

I wanted the meetings to evolve in response to what happened rather then having a clear format from the beginning. They took various forms. Meeting one was to introduce the project and discuss ethical issues. Meetings two and three provided the opportunity to focus on the children's mark making at home. Meetings four and six were workshops in which the children participated and meeting five provided time to reflect on the Art Workshop. The final meeting was planned to give us time to talk about recent events and to consolidate our learning about provision in the home for mark making.

At the first meeting I asked the participants how they defined mark making. One mother's comment was that it is a 'politically correct term for drawing'; another that 'It's about him making his mark in the world'. This second comment captured our imaginations and we started to consider different situations where children make marks. Some of the suggestions were: on car windows, making footprints in the snow, walking through puddles, in dough and gloop, hammering into wood, in jelly, food and in polystyrene. This discussion opened all our minds to endless possibilities. The parents agreed to be 'mark making spotters' and to write down what their children said as they made their various marks.

Focused conversation

The following focused conversation describes Alice's, Rebecca's and Ellie's learning at home as reported by their mothers.

Mary and Alice (age 4:2)

Lillian: Looks like a map, (see Figure 1).

Mary: Exactly what she said. What did you say that was? She was doing a lot of ladders. She's always drawing, she adds up now, she says three add three is ...but when she gets to six add six! She's got two older brothers, so if they're doing their homework she's ...She goes on the computer.

This was just one of eleven examples. Mary, Alice's mother said that materials were always available for Alice to use in many ways. Alice demonstrated an interest in connections, making marks using different media, including pens and the computer. Her older siblings provided positive role models.

Amanda and Rebecca (age 4:1)

Rebecca had responded to Amanda's suggestion that she draw a picture of her family (see Figure 2).

Amanda: She started with herself in the middle, which I thought she would. As she was drawing she said, 'acrobatic legs.' She said it was

Figure 1

Figure 2

me as a child but she denied it later. She did these dots. You don't realise how much is going on in her mind. I found it fascinating, you don't realise. When I did the first one (observation) I got hooked on it.

This is an extract from Amanda's observation:

While she drew there was a constant running commentary, so what I recorded was probably less than a quarter of what she said.

Counted fingers as she drew them. As she was drawing legs she said:

Rebecca: Mum, I'm playing hobblesticks on this picture. I've got bare toes because everyone has to have bare toes to play fiddle-balance. Shall I do it a sunny day or a rainy day?

Rebecca decided to do a snowy day (it had been snowing earlier). Drew snow before colouring her jumper and trousers. Was going to do a black jumper with patterns, but when I suggested that a pattern wouldn't show on top of black as it was felt-tip, not paint, she decided on plain black.

Rebecca: I'm writing names, now I've got to do dots. Dotty is its name. I'm going to do a floating 'A' for Amanda. Actually that would spoil the picture. I'm doing my family.

She asked what colour trousers I would like and drew my feet, saying:

Rebecca: One toe sticking out of that trouser leg, two toes sticking out of that trouser leg. Mum what else would you like?

Meaning what else would I like to wear. She drew her own bobble hat after drawing me, counting the bobbles as she drew them.

Rebecca: Me and you have got plain blue hats with bobbles.

Then followed some conversation about Nigel's spiky hat. She drew a dot on the right hand side.

Rebecca: Mum, do you know what that's going to be?

Amanda: No I don't.

She drew a series of dots, then pointed at them in turn saying,

Figure 3

Rebecca: Baby, child, child, child, child, child, child, mummy, daddy. The mummy and daddy have got one baby, one child, two child, three child, four child, five child, six child, one mummy and one daddy. They're a family of bubbles. Do you know who is blowing these bubbles? Nigel!

She drew Nigel under the bubbles. Nigel is disabled and can't stand up without support, but interestingly she always draws him standing, even though he's nearly always in his wheelchair, sitting on the floor, or chair or when upstairs crawling. Next she drew daddy, but calling him Ernest as she drew him.

Rebecca: It's all finished.

I asked her if she would like another piece of paper and she replied:

Rebecca: Actually, I am bored of drawing

Figure 4

...and put the felt-tips away.

Amanda found the experience of scribing Rebecca's talk enlightening and as she says, 'fascinating.' Amanda elaborated on Rebecca's theory about her brother, Nigel:

> *She's into the family. This is Nigel. (See figure 3.) She's drawn Nigel about three or four times. Twice she said he's on tip toes, he doesn't stand. I've asked the other children not to say anything because I want to know when she draws Nigel in a wheelchair for the first time.*

Amanda has identified Rebecca's theory about her older brother's physical disability. She states the relationship between Rebecca's understandings as represented through her drawing and awaits changes as an indication of developments in Rebecca's learning. The foci in these observations are the search for meanings and the relevance of the social context.

Sonia and Ellie (age 3:10)

Ellie also responded to the suggestion that she draw a picture of her family (see figure 4.) This is Sonia's observation.

Ellie: This is you mummy, growing your hair. I'm just writing your name. Now I'm gonna do me.

Ellie draws her fingers.

Ellie: One, two, three, four, five. Now I'm gonna draw you Melissa. What has it got on your jumper? Does doggy doggy need four legs? I did a body. Right, I need to see what it says.

Ellie copies the letters from the T-shirt.

Ellie: You've got your hair Melissa right down to here.

Ellie counts fingers.

Ellie: One, two three, four, five. This is you Melissa. Melissa can write your name here. I'm going to draw Matthew.

Sonia: Why is Matthew smaller?

Ellie: 'Cos he is eight. Daddy now.

Sonia: Why is daddy smaller?

Ellie: Just need to do it down there, cos I've run out of room. Daddy is thirty eight. Done it. Now Dog. Dog has one eye, one, two, three, four, legs. Just need to do the fishes. There they both are. Just need to do them things (meaning fins). Done it now. No, just need to do some flowers. I'll just do some stars and a sun. Done it!

It is evident from Ellie's running commentary that she draws each family member methodically. She counts confidently to ensure the details are accurate and she involves those around her. Ellie is able to reason and can offer an explanation for why dad is smaller.

These extracts, typical of the many recorded in the mothers' transcriptions of their children's talk, reveal the complexities of the children's theories. They also demonstrate the value of asking parents to focus in dialogue with professionals on aspects of their children's learning.

The evaluation process

I used two questionnaires to evaluate the series of focused conversations with this group of parents. The outcomes are summarised here. The first consisted of two questions: 'What have you learnt about children's mark making?' and 'What have you learnt about your child?' These questions focused on my second research question 'What will participants learn about their children and their children's mark making?'

The questionnaire data confirm that from the first meeting the participants had adopted a broad definition of mark making. As Lillian explained, 'children use all things to make marks which reflect the world around them.' Mandy described 'shadows, raindrops on pavements and steamy windows' as presenting opportunities for children to make marks. The parents expressed their heightened appreciation of the children's mark making and a shared understanding of the value of the earliest marks. The participation of Joshua, a two-year old sibling, enriched the work, allowing us to observe a two-year-old in action. His mother Sonia said, 'I have discovered these marks, that is, scribbling, marking in sand, footprints are all essential stages a child needs to progress through in order to become an emergent writer.' The parents reinforced their role in supporting and encouraging their children, providing the appropriate materials and opportunities for mark making. The parents were asked what they had learned about their own children. Themes of appreciation and understanding recur in such comments as:

I have been able to enter her imagination and see the world through her eyes.

Now I'm fascinated by the way she develops a drawing, rather than just looking at the end result.

I have learnt that Brandon is more capable of mark making than I first thought.

This last statement emphasises the need for practitioners to share their knowledge of the children so that parents are better placed to enjoy, enhance and extend their children's learning.

A second questionnaire was used to evaluate the success of the focus group. The first question asked the parents to rank each initiative in terms of very useful, useful, not useful and don't know. Table two shows an overview of the evaluation outcomes.

Analysis of this first question shows that all the processes initiated were perceived as very useful or useful. The most popular aspect of the project was an Art Workshop and the parents most enjoyed activities that involved watching their children. The experience of running the workshops and evaluating them confirms the success of the group and provides the impetus to move on and initiate parent focus groups in the future.

Conclusion and recommendations

This small scale study has demonstrated that the children and parents involved engaged in a variety of mark making activities in their homes. The parents see mark making as a worthwhile activity to be encouraged. The parents learned from observing their children and developed an appreciation of their children's high levels of involvement, discussing their children's achievements at home with confidence, clarity and joy.

The future

In our school we shall repeat the process described here throughout the school year in order to involve more parents. Issues of equality

Table Two: Participants' Rankings of activities

Activity	Very useful	Useful	Not useful	Don't know
Discussions about mark making	3	3		
Discussions about other school issues	3	3		
Looking at children's work	3	3		
Observing your own child	4	2		
Writing down what your child said	4	2		
The Art Workshop in the Family Room	5	1		
The video of the Art Workshop	3	1		2
The Visit to the Art Gallery	3	1		2
The Writing Activity (stages of development)	3	3		
Filling in the grid about strands of mark making	2	4		

of opportunity need to be addressed and I plan to encourage the involvement of other colleagues and of fathers as well as mothers. A flexible planning format needs to be retained to facilitate the response to needs and ideas. The popularity of the workshop sessions is evident in the participants' evaluations so they could be developed further.

For our setting, parent focus groups can become an integral part of what we do and a means of ensuring the involvement of more parents. Opportunities for action research can be utilised as a method for professional development amongst colleagues and we shall further disseminate our experiences by inviting participants to return and talk with parents new to the school of their experiences.

The children have been the primary beneficiaries of this collaboration between parents and practitioners. We all had valuable knowledge and understanding to share. This was a group which enjoyed mutual respect, shared understandings, political awareness and a commitment to extending learning opportunities for young children.

References

Abbott, L. (1997), 'A curriculum for the under threes – definitions and provision' in Abbott, L., Ackers, J., Gillen, J., Grant-Mullings., Griffin, B and Marsh, C. *Educare For The Under Threes – Identifying need and opportunity*, paper Presented at 7th European Early Childhood Education research AssociationConference, Munich, Germany, 3rd – 6th September, 1997

Arnold, C. (2001) , 'Persistence pays off: working with 'hard to reach' parents' in Whalley, M. and the Pen Green Centre Team (2001), *Involving Parents in Their Children's Learning*, London: Paul Chapman Publishing, p96-116

Athey, C. (1990), *Extending Thought in Young Children, a parent – teacher partnership* London: Paul Chapman Publishing

Clough, P. and Nutbrown, C. (2002) *A Students' Guide to Methodology: justifying enquiry* London: Sage

Cohen, L., Manion, L. and Morrison, K. (2000, 5th ed) *Research Methods in Education* London: RoutledgeFalmer

Dahlberg, G., Moss, P. and Pence, A. (1999, ed.) *Beyond Quality in Early Childhood Education and Care: postmodern perspectives* London: RoutledgeFalmer

Graue, M. E., and Walsh, D. J. (1998), *Studying Children in Context: theories, methods and ethics* London: SAGE

Hannon, P. and Nutbrown, C. (2001) Working with Parents on Early Literacy Development: emerging findings. Paper presented at the annual conference of the British Educational Research Association University of Leeds, September 2001

Malaguzzi, L. (1998), 'History, ideas, and basic philosophy: an interview with Lella Gandini' in Edwards, Gandini and Forman (ed) *The Hundred Languages of Children, the Reggio Emilia approach – advanced reflections* London: JAI Press Limited, pp49-97

Marsh, J. (2000), 'Ethical issues in early childhood education', Module 4, Unit 9, p1-17, *Diploma/MA In Early Childhood Education*, Sheffield: University of Sheffield Department of Educational Studies

Nutbrown, C. and Hannon, P. (eds) (1997) *Preparing for Literacy Education with Parents: a professional development manual*, Sheffield/Nottingham: University of Sheffield/NES Arnold

Nutbrown, C. (1999a, 2nd ed) *Threads of Thinking: young children learning and the role of early education* London: Paul Chapman Publishing

Nutbrown, C. (1999b), 'Parents' roles in children's learning', Module 2, Unit 9, p1-5, *Diploma/MA In Early Childhood Education,* Sheffield: University of Sheffield Department of Educational Studies

Nutbrown, C. (2002), 'Focused conversations and focus groups' In Clough, P. and Nutbrown, C. (2002) *A Students' Guide to Methodology: justifying enquiry* London: Sage

Parker, C. (2001), 'She's back! The impact of my visit to Reggio Emilia on a group of 3- and 4- year-olds' In Abbott, L. and Nutbrown, C., (eds.) *Experiencing Reggio Emilia: implications for pre-school provision* Buckingham: Open University Press, p80-92

Qualifications and Curriculum Authority. (2000) *Curriculum Guidance for the Foundation Stage* London: QCA

Rennie, J. (1996), 'Working with parents' In Pugh, G. *Contemporary Issues in the Early Years: working collaboratively for children* (2nd ed), London: Paul Chapman Publishing, p189- 208

Rinaldi, C. (1998), 'Projected curriculum constructed through documentation – *progettazione*: an interview with Lella Gandini' in Edwards, Gandini and Forman (ed.) *The Hundred Languages of Children, the Reggio Emilia approach – advanced reflections* London: JAI Press p113-126

Tizard, B. and Hughes, M (1981) *Young Children Learning* London: Fulton

Weinberger, J. (1997) *Literacy Goes to School* London: Paul Chapman Publishing

Whalley, M. and the Pen Green Centre Team (2001) *Involving Parents in their Children's Learning*, London: Paul Chapman Publishing p74-95.

8

Preschool writing development and the role of parents

Anne Kirkpatrick

Overview

This chapter reports a study to describe and document the home writing experiences of eight preschool children from a range of families over an eighteen-month period. More specifically, I wanted to know:

- Is there any evidence of writing development?

- What kind of development is there?

- How much variation in development is there within the sample?

- Does parental involvement affect children's writing development?

The writing development of each child in the sample was monitored and aspects of development were identified. These included an increasing understanding of purposes for writing, writing conventions and growing independence. Variation in development among the eight children was also examined, and was found to be largely a result of differing literacy practices and levels of parental involvement.

The study was undertaken as part of a larger research programme which aimed to raise parents' awareness of the importance of their role in their children's early literacy development (The REAL

(Raising Early Achievement in Literacy) Project, Hannon and Nutbrown, 2001). As a member of the REAL Project team, I worked with eight families for eighteen months. Children were aged just three at the beginning of the project.

Each family was asked to collect examples of their child's writing and drawings in a scrapbook. In addition, I made notes of every visit to each family kept a journal which included observations and records of conversations. Writing samples produced by the children during home visits were also collected. The children were assessed at the beginning and end of the project using the British Picture Vocabulary Scale (Dunn *et al.*, 1997) and the Sheffield Early Literacy Development Profile (SELDP; Nutbrown, 1997). Some of the SELDP assessment data has been used in this study alongside the analysis of the writing samples, since it was judged to provide a complementary perspective on development.

The methods used in this study include a combination of participant observation, unstructured observations and discussions, standardised assessment data and analysis of written samples, produced both as part of home visits and independently. The combination of these objective and subjective methods enabled me to obtain a full picture of the children's writing development.

Consistent with other research, this study found that many parents are initiating and engaging in literacy activities with their children. In some cases, REAL Project intervention programme (Nutbrown and Hannon, 1997) appeared to increase the frequency and quality of home writing experiences. One of the most significant findings of the study reported in this chapter was that parental involvement strongly influenced the children's progress. However, an over-emphasis on letter formation and correct spelling (towards the end of the project) appeared to have a negative effect on some children's confidence.

Introduction: locating the study in the literature

Research has shown that home environment is a source of experiences that can enhance the development of literacy (Bissex, 1980; Schickedanz, 1990). However, the majority of studies into preschool literacy development have tended to focus on reading and adult-child book sharing; writing has largely been overlooked. There have been some useful studies of preschool writing development, although most have tended to take place in nursery settings (Clay, 1975; Ferreiro and Teberosky, 1982; Harste, Woodward and Burke, 1984). This may be significant as it is generally acknowledged that there are vast differences between literacy practices children experience at home and those they are introduced to when they enter school (Tizard and Hughes, 1984; Hall, 1987). At home, children are involved in 'real' literacy activities which are enjoyable, not just functional on an information exchanging or task performing level. In contrast, at school, activities are often contrived and appear to be for no apparent purpose.

Most studies (Clay, 1975; Ferreiro and Teberosky, 1982; Harste, Woodward and Burke, 1984) focused on children aged five and above. The very early stages of writing have been largely ignored. Studying three to five year old children's writing acquisition may offer some insight into the crucial early stages of writing development and the way in which children begin to make sense of writing conventions.

While there have been case studies of an individual child's development at home over a number of years (e.g. Bissex, 1980; Schickedanz, 1990), few researchers have looked at the development of several children's writing over a relatively long period. There is a need for longitudinal research because often children's writing development does not occur in a straightforward, stage-like development from immature form to more mature form, as suggested by Ferreiro and Teberosky (1982). Sometimes children seem to go back and forth across different forms of writing.

Parents' contributions to their children's literacy acquisition are now recognised as crucial (Dickinson, 1994; Hannon, 1995). However, although many parents try to help their preschool aged children in their acquisition of literacy, they do so in different ways, to varying degrees, and with different concepts of literacy (Heath, 1983; Taylor and Dorsey-Gaines, 1988; Hannon et al., 1991). There have been a number of studies into the effects of preschool adult-child shared reading, but the role of parents in children's writing acquisition has received far less attention. Studying the development of several children in home settings would enable variations in parental contributions to be gauged. Comparisons between children and their range of backgrounds could also be made.

Is there any evidence of writing development?

In the study reported here there was evidence of development, although the amount and type of development varied with each child in the sample. In this section, writing samples from two of the eight children in the sample are discussed. These particular two were selected as they illustrate contrasting development.

Figure 1(a) to 1(e) shows Lucy's writing, produced independently – apart from the first sample, which was produced after watching her mother write, and the last, which was part of a home visit, although little prompting was involved. There is obvious development between the first and last samples. In the first 1(a), she filled the lines with the same form: mainly zigzagged lines with some circular shapes. 1(b) is a list written from left to right and top to bottom and, although none of the marks are recognisable as letters, different types of mark have been used, with a mixture of circular and straight lines. Figure 1(c) consists of letters and letter-like shapes. Figure 1(d) shows greater pencil control and a greater variety of letters. Finally, in sample 1(e) Lucy was beginning to assign sounds to the letters, and was able to write 'ro.ls.ct' (roller skates) as part of her Christmas list.

Mitchell's samples also (show development) see Figures 2(a) to 2(c) although there was a long period in which few samples were obtained. However, there was clear development between ages 3:9 and 4:8. At age 3:9 (Figure 2(a)), he was using a combination of circular and straight lines, with little apparent control. By age 4:8, (Figure 2(b)), he was attempting to write his name, with some success. Two months later, at age 4:10, (Figure 2(c)), he was clearly beginning to assign sounds to letters. This piece was produced on a home visit.

What is the nature of writing development at home?

Writing samples obtained showed development in terms of:

- understanding purposes for writing
- perceptions of writing
- independence

Figure 1: Lucy's Writing Development

1(a) Book Review-age 3:3

1(b) List – age 3:3

1 (c) Letters and numbers – age 3:10

1(d) Letters, numbers and name-age 4:6

1(e) 'Roller skates' – age 4:7

Figure 2: Mitchell's writing development

2(a) Drawing – age 3:9   2 (b) Name writing – age 4:8

2 (c) 'b for boy' – age 4:10

Figure 3: Menu (Lucy age 3:8)

- writing conventions
- influence of reading on writing
- understanding phonics

Development of understanding the purposes for writing

There was evidence that over the eighteen-month research period the children – and their parents – developed their understanding of the purposes for writing. At the start, few parents reported that their children wrote in role-play or for other purposes. A few had encouraged their children to write their names into birthday and other occasion cards, but only one mother said that she encouraged her son to write for other purposes, for example, by writing shopping lists with her.

After four months of the project, I held a workshop for parents on writing development. The purpose was to explain the stages of writing development, to raise parents' awareness about what type of

Figure 4: Drawing
(Lucy age 3:2)

writing to encourage and how they could become involved by setting up a variety of writing scenarios with their children at home.

After the workshop, different types of writing began to appear in the scrapbooks. Previously, the writing had tended to focus on letter formation and copy writing but evidence of writing for different purposes increased. Either the children were increasingly engaged in these different types of writing contexts, or their parents were now recognising them as important and collecting the samples in scrapbooks.

An example of writing for a purpose can be seen in Figure 3, Lucy's menu was produced as a result of role-play with her mother.

Writing perceptions

At a very young age, Lucy understood the difference between writing and drawing. Figure 4 is a pencil drawing of a person (age 3:2) with a quite separate 'caption', consisting mainly of semi-circles and straight lines, written at its side.

Mitchell had different perceptions of writing, however. On a home visit when he was aged 4:8, I asked him to help Polly, my bear puppet, to write a list of things she would need for her party. He began to draw, starting from the right hand side of the page and working towards the left (see Figure 5). 'That's a apple. That's a pear. That's a orange. That's a banana,' he said as he drew each object in turn. He then drew a figure. 'That's Polly,' he said, 'That's me, and that's you,' (the figure with spiky hair). He finished by writing his name at the right hand side of the paper.

Figure 5: Polly's party list (Mitchell age 4:8)

Mitchell had possibly not understood what was required of him when he was asked to write as part of a specific task. He may have assumed that writing was the same as drawing.

Development of independence

The samples show a developing independence over time, in that the children became less reliant upon adults and on copywriting. At first, many of the parents would draw faint alphabetic letters for their children to trace. Such 'copy writing' arguably does not encourage independence and confidence in young children's writing capabilities, especially when used in isolation, not in conjunction with other methods. Virtually all the parents in the sample were encouraging their children to write solely in this way, and many children seemed to lack confidence in their own ability to 'write' independently.

Some of the children were involved in writing activities independent of their parents, usually with older siblings. Nicole's mother reported that she and her brother would often engage in role-play. At first, Nicole's older brother would always take the writing role of waiter, doctor or shopkeeper. As time went on, however, Nicole began to take the writing role, bullying her brother into other roles!

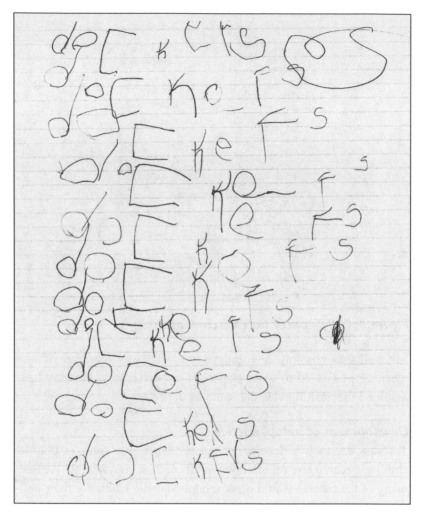

Figure 6: Dockers (Sophie age 4:7)

Development of writing conventions
Letter formation and pencil control
Lucy and Mitchell's writing samples show clear development in terms of letter formation and pencil control (Figures 1 and 2). The other children in the sample showed similar development.

Spelling
In addition to developing skills of letter formation, some children in the sample began to write certain words they knew how to spell correctly on many of their writings and drawings. Most often this was

Figure 7: 'The Very Hungry Caterpillar' (Ryan age 4:1)

their name, although one child had a more complex word in her repertoire. Sophie was very excited that she would be getting some red Dr. Martens boots for Christmas and had asked her mother to write the word 'dockers' for her to copy. She had copied it so many times that she was able to write it from memory and proudly presented me with a page of A4 filled with the word 'dockers' (see figure 6). This is an example of what Ferreiro and Teberosky (1982) term a 'stable string', in which a child writes a word he/she knows how to spell over and over.

Lines

Nathan provided an example of how children become aware of writing conventions, by demonstrating his understanding of the way adults, and older children, use lines. He had produced a page of 'writing', then proceeded to draw lines across, separating it and saying, *'There. That's to stop the writing going into each other.'*

Development of the effect of reading on writing

This refers to how the print children see around them every day, such as environmental print or books, affects their writing. In the study

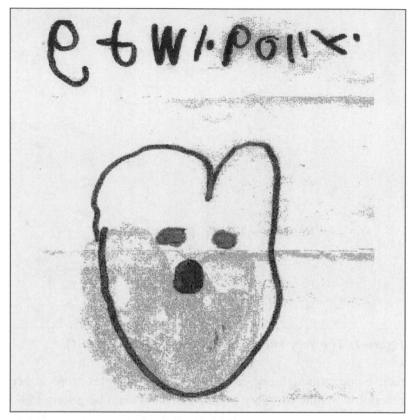

Figure 8: Polly's 'Get Well' card (Lucy age 4:7)

samples, there were only limited examples of such influences. The strongest influences appeared to be from the books borrowed by the children at the end of each visit, and took the form of drawings rather than writing. Figure 7 is typical and shows a pencil drawing of *The Very Hungry Caterpillar* by Eric Carle. Occasionally the children's pictures from the books were accompanied by some writing copied from them.

Development of an understanding of phonics
By the end of the research period, some of the children were beginning to use phonics to help them write certain words. At age 4:7, Lucy wrote a get well card for my puppet; 'gtwl.polly' (get well Polly) as part of a home visit, see Figure 8.

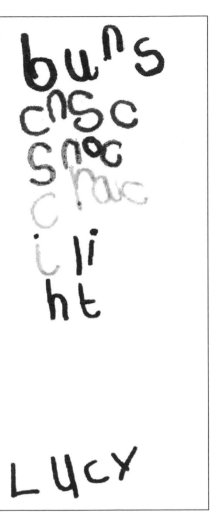

Figure 9: Polly's Party List (Lucy age 4:8)

Lucy used a dot rather than a space between 'wl' and 'polly'. A few weeks later, she wrote a list of things needed for Polly the puppet's party (Figure 9). On this occasion, she wrote without any hesitation at all, and was able to sound out all the letters in 'buns'. A little re-assurance was given to write the other things on the list; 'cnsc' (Christmas cake), 'snoc' (sand-wiches), 'jli' (jelly) and 'ht' (hats). Lucy started writing each word underneath the previous one with-out being instructed to do so, probably because she knew this was the form a list should take. Having seen her mother write shopping lists, she knew that they usually took the form of words written beneath one another.

Rates of development in writing varied from child to child, and while all children showed some development, not all showed every type of development discussed here. This brings us to the next question.

How much variation in writing development is there within the sample?

Some differences between the children's development have already been identified. However, it was felt that an objective method of assessment was also needed in order to determine the extent of any differences. All children in the project were assessed at the beginning and end of the project using the SELDP (Nutbrown, 1997).

Table 1 shows the writing scores at the beginning and end of the project, but it is each child's development, or the 'difference' in writing, that this study is particularly concerned with. The two children for whom there is no data would not co-operate for the first assessment. Lucy and Sophie showed the greatest development in writing over the two-year period, followed by Harry and Nathan, with John and Mitchell showing the least.

	Writing January 1887	Writing December 1998	Difference
Lucy	3	13	10
Sophie	2	14	12
Nicole	No data	9	No data
Nathan	3	10	7
Mitchell	2	6	4
Ryan	No data	7	No data
Harry	3	10	7
John	5	9	4
Maximum 20 points			
Source: REAL Project data			

Table 1: Writing Scores SELDP

In addition to the assessment results in Table 1, another method which allows us to look at the children's differing rates of development in more detail has been used. This involves noting the different times that certain letters first appeared in the children's writing. Graphs were drawn to illustrate the development. The first, Figure 10, shows the number of letters each of the children was using independently, for example in their playwriting, at particular ages. Unfortunately, there were not enough samples from John or Harry to work from.

Lucy showed the most development over the eighteen-month period. At age 3:2 she was using four letters, and by age 4:7 she was using seventeen. Sophie and Ryan also showed rapid development, beginning around age 4:5. Nathan's development was steadier, although he was using thirteen letters by age 4:11.

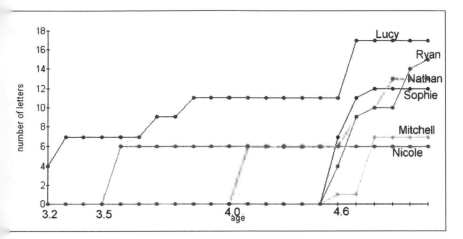

Figure 10: Graph to show first independent use of letters
(Source: Study Data)

The second graph, Figure 11, shows first appearance of letters copied from an adult. It is therefore a useful tool for examining such issues as parental involvement. This graph also includes letters copied from, for example, environmental print, posters or books at the child's own initiative. Again, Lucy showed most development: by age 3:10 she had copied all the letters of the alphabet in lower case. Nicole also showed good progress around age 4:0, and this continued to age 4:11. This was in contrast to her independent use of letters, which was much more limited. There was little evidence of copy writing in the samples for Ryan and Mitchell. This is interesting, particularly in the case of Ryan, who showed good independent development from around age 4:5. Mitchell too, began to write the letters from his name independently around this age; by age 4:11 he was using seven letters.

Does parental involvement affect children's writing development?

The purpose of the REAL Project was to raise *parents'* awareness about the importance of their role in their children's development. The parents were asked to follow up the home visit with specific literacy activities. The amount of involvement varied enormously across the eight families. One or two did everything suggested to

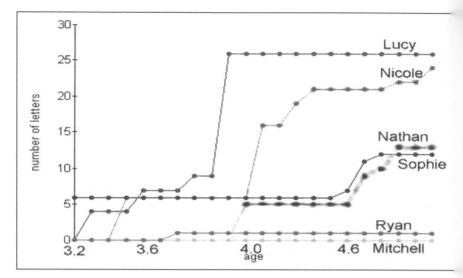

Figure 11: Graph to show first copied use of letters
(Source: Study data)

them and more, whereas two or three families just read the books borrowed with their children.

Following the writing development workshop, more parents began to collect their children's early writing, and most included play-writing samples in the scrapbooks. As time went on however, some parents once again began stressing the importance of correct letter formation and copied words, and consequently, some of the children seemed to lose the confidence to play-write in the presence of adults.

Lucy, Harry and Nicole's parents were very involved and always completed the follow-up activities. Both Lucy and Harry knew all letter sounds by the end of the project and Lucy was beginning to write independently. Harry however, seemed inhibited by his fear of 'getting it wrong' and lacked confidence to write independently.

Nicole's mother was desperately trying to teach Nicole letter sounds. '*I keep trying*' she said, '*but Nicole just isn't interested. Give her toys and she'll concentrate for hours, but with this she gets bored after a few minutes.*' John's mother, a teacher, was an advocate of 'emergent literacy'. John was a bright boy who knew all letter sounds by the end of the project. He was also articulate, and enjoyed looking at and discussing books. John's mother often tried to encourage her son to play-write, without success. Although his mother had never been over concerned about spelling, John, like Harry and Nicole, had developed a fear of 'getting it wrong'. John's mother said:

> *His writing's got to look like writing; it's got to be proper words. If he's not copying my writing, or writing from a book, the only word he'll write is his name, because he knows how to spell that!*

Future research

This study provided an exploration of some factors that can contribute to very young children's writing development at home. There is scope for further research in this under-researched area.

Harste, Woodward and Burke (1984) found that some children were willing to experiment with literacy even if this meant making mistakes. These 'risk-takers' were found to be better language learners. In this study, at least three of the children lacked confidence in their own writing ability. Two of the eight were, to a certain extent, risk takers and these were children who were making good progress with writing. Future studies could further investigate the behaviours of 'risk takers' as compared with less confident literacy learners, and attempt to identify factors that may contribute to such confidence.

While one of the main conclusions of this study was that parental involvement is very important in young children's early writing development, it is possible that for certain children an over emphasis on the importance of letter formation and spelling may have a detrimental effect on their confidence. Future studies could investigate this further.

References

Bissex, G. (1980) *GYNS AT WRK: A child learns to write and read*. Cambridge, MA: Harvard University Press

Clay, M. M. (1975) *What did I write?* Auckland, New Zealand: Heinemann Educational

Dickinson, D.K. (1994) (Ed.) *Bridges to literacy: children, families and schools* Cambridge, MA: Blackwell

Dunn, L.M., Whetton, C. and Burley, J. (1997) *The British Picture Vocabulary Scale – second edition*. Slough: NFER-Nelson

Ferreiro, E. and Teberosky, A. (1982) *Literacy before schooling*. Portsmouth, NH: Heinemann

Hall, N. (1987). *The emergence of literacy* London: Hodder and Stoughton

Hannon, P. (1995) *Literacy home and school: research and practice in teaching literacy with parents*. London: Falmer

Hannon, P. and Nutbrown, C. (2001) *Working with Parents on Early Literacy Development: emerging findings.* Paper presented at the annual conference of the British Educational Research Association University of Leeds, September 2001

Hannon, P., Weinberger, J. and Nutbrown, C. (1991) A study of work with parents to promote early literacy development *Research Papers in Education*, 6, 2, 77-97

Harste, J.C., Woodward, V.A., and Burke, C.L. (1984) *Language Stories and Literacy Lessons* Portsmouth, NH: Heinemann

Heath, S.B. (1983) *Ways with words: Language, life and work in communities and classrooms* Cambridge: Cambridge University Press

Nutbrown, C. (1997) *Recognising Early Literacy Development: assessing children's achievements.* London: Paul Chapman Publishing

Nutbrown, C. and Hannon, P. (editors) (1997) *Preparing For Literacy Education With Parents: A professional development manual,* Sheffield/Nottingham: University of Sheffield/NES Arnold

Schickedanz, J. (1990). *Adam's Righting Revolutions* Portsmouth NH: Heinemann

Taylor, D., and Dorsey Gaines, C. (1988) *Emergent Literacy: writing and reading.* Norwood NJ: Ablex

Tizard, B. and Hughes, M. (1984) *Young children learning: Talking and thinking at home and in school.* London: Falmer

Part 2

WORKING WITH DIFFERENCE AND DIVERSITY IN PRESCHOOL SETTINGS

9

Understanding gender issues in preschool settings

Vicky Grant

Introduction

In recent years my professional interest in boys' apparent social dominance in a preschool setting has led me to study issues of social and gender dominance. In this chapter I report the development of a small-scale study of the role models portrayed by parents and their relation to different social and economic factors. For the purposes of this study, three preschool settings were selected in and around Edinburgh: a Nursery School in a Scottish Borders Town outside Edinburgh (setting A), a Nursery School in an inner city area of low employment and poor housing (Setting B), and a Nursery Class in one of the Edinburgh's more affluent suburbs. The research used a questionnaire survey of parents from six families from each of the three settings and an interview with the preschool children in these families.

Ethical considerations in the research

I wanted to find out parents' opinions on gender roles and what sort of gender role model they felt they were providing for their children. I also decided to interview their children in order to investigate the impact of these role models in terms of how the children responded to the gender-career role models their parents provided. To select the sample group, three different settings in and around Edinburgh were chosen, to reflect different socio-economic backgrounds so that I could interpret the findings in terms of social class. I used a short questionnaire to elicit parents' responses. No family names were used and a coding system ensured that their responses remained confidential, protected from identification by the nursery staff who had day-to-day contact with them. A system of colour coding made it possible to co-ordinate the parents' and children's responses and so analyse data family by family as well as setting by setting.

I developed a simple schedule for interviews with the children, which included some picture prompts to hold their attention and make data collection flexible and enjoyable for them

Confidentiality

The co-operation of the staff in the setting was especially important in the research, as was building up a strong relationship of trust and confidentiality between the Nursery Teachers, myself and the parents involved. The research questionnaire contained requested personal information, so it was important to be able to assure the parents that the Nursery Teacher would not see the results of the questionnaire and that I would not know the names of the families.

Each family was given two colour-coded copies of the questionnaire (matching the colour given by the teacher), a corresponding coloured envelope and a covering letter explaining the requirements of the research. The letter explained the colour coding of the questionnaires and asked each parent to fill in their questionnaire on their own and give it, in a sealed envelope, to one of the nursery staff, who returned it to me. Thus the nursery staff who knew the parents involved had no access to the completed questionnaires and the families were assured of anonymity and confidentiality. A similar process was used to anonymise the interviews with the children and enable their responses to be matched to those of their parents.

Methodological issues
Choosing the families

In selecting the families to be interviewed, I relied on the knowledge of the teachers in each setting and asked them to approach the families they had chosen from their different settings and distribute the questionnaires; two questionnaires to each family, one for each parent. I chose this approach because in the area of low employment there was a high level of adult literacy difficulty and I wanted to avoid embarrassment for any parents who might find it difficult to complete a written questionnaire. Additionally, I wanted six families from each of the settings, three families with a boy in the nursery and three families with a girl, eighteen families in total. I also requested that the questionnaires be distributed to families where both parents lived in the same household so that the opinions of both the male and female role model in the home could be obtained. I considered this important as the home provides the child with their first major influence of gender role models. Further studies could investigate the impact of gender roles on children living with lone parents.

The questionnaire to parents

The questionnaire consisted of two parts and had both open and closed questions. The first section covered questions on their children's toy preferences and asked for the parents' views on what they felt were unsuitable toys for their children to play with. The second part asked for personal information on education, employment and family background. When considering the request for sensitive and personal material in the questionnaire, it is important to view the questions through the eyes of the respondents, since questions that might appear innocent to the researcher could be regarded as highly sensitive or offensive to the respondent (Cohen *et al.*, 2000, p257). Consequently, I decided not to ask the parents to allocate themselves to a socio-economic group by number, but to deduce such information from their responses to more subtly tailored questions. Distinct differences in education and employment were shown between the three families in each of the three settings.

Interviews with children

The interview with children was fairly brief and asked them about their favourite toys, what they didn't like playing with, what they liked playing with, what they want to be when they grew up and what their parents did when they went to work. This last question sought to establish whether the parents acted as such a strong role model that they influenced the child's choice of career. Children were also shown a series of pictures representing various jobs and asked if a man or a woman would do those jobs – such as a police constable, fire fighter, vet, nurse and doctor. Finally, the children were shown pictures of toys and asked if they could choose four toys that boys would like to play with and four toys that girls would like to play with. This question tended to take longest to answer as children poured over the pictures of toys, saying which ones they had or wanted or were getting for Christmas!

Worth remembering when interviewing children is the fact that some children will say *anything* rather than nothing at all, thereby limiting the possible reliability of the data (see Simons, 1982 and Lewis, 1992). This was evident when one child indicated that he would like to be a rabbit when he grew up!

Response rate
Due to the co-operation of nursery staff and parents, most questionnaires were returned promptly and only a few had to be chased up by the nursery staff after the requested submission date. Due to the relatively small numbers taking part in the research in each setting and the fact that the Nursery Teachers kept a note of the families involved, all questionnaires were completed and handed in, resulting in a 100% response rate from both parents and children

Some findings
Data from the parents and children were analysed together so as to gain a picture of their views as a whole family. Quantitative data were analysed, providing a quantitative overview of families on a setting by setting basis and the more qualitative responses were sifted and categorised to provide more detailed pictures of what lay beneath the statistics.

In setting A, the six children in the sample group attended a nursery in a peripheral housing scheme. On the whole, their parents' school-leaving age was low, unemployment levels were high and further education was rare and focused on college based courses with no University level education. These findings are indicative of the reputation of the area, as having low employment and poor housing. Parents using Setting B, a nursery class in a more affluent suburb of Edinburgh and Setting C, a nursery class in a Border town outside Edinburgh, both revealed similar circumstances: school leaving age was higher; parents had achieved more school qualifications (than parents using Setting A) before gaining, in the main, university degrees. Employment levels in the families from settings B and C were high.

In informal interviews the children were asked what they would like to do when they grew up. In Settings B and C all but one of the children were aware of their parents' careers, but this did not appear to influence them when it came to suggesting their own future career choices. Although not acting as role models in influencing potential career choices, the parents seem to be providing a model of working parents that encourages their children to think about what they want to be when they grow up.

This is in contrast to the children in Setting A, where parents from three of the six families were unemployed. Five of the six children in the sample group were unsure of what their parents did at work and three of them did not know what they wanted to be when they grew up. Admittedly, these children are very young and likely to change their minds many, many times before choosing a career but the key point here is the heightened awareness - and therefore possibly greater opportunity – of children from families in a higher socio-economic group.

The survey suggests no discernable distinction between the children in each of the Settings with regard to gender roles and how they are affected by different social and economic factors. If anything, comparisons could be made with regard to the social backgrounds of the families in Setting B and Setting C.

Some Implications for Practice

This research throws up one major implication for practice. If some children learn negative gender stereotypes at home, early childhood provision must provide a broader view with a wider vision of gender roles and opportunities for all. Early Childhood Educators have responsibility to promote positive gender role models through day-to-day activities, whatever children's family or community circumstances, but perhaps this is particularly important where views of family and community appear to narrow vision and opportunity.

References

Cohen, L., Manion, L. and Morrison, K. (2000) *Research Methods in Education* London: RoutledgeFalmer

Lewis, A. (1992) 'Group child interviews as a research tool, *British Educational Research Journal,* 18 (4), 413-21

Simons, H. (1982) 'Conversation piece: the practice of interviewing in case study research' in McCormick, R. (ed.) *Calling Education to Account* London: Heinemann, p 239-46

10

Gender roles and toys in the home: parents' attitudes and children's experiences

Nicky Walters

Frogs and snails and puppy dogs' tails
that's what little boys are made of
Sugar and spice and all things nice
That's what little girls are made of.

Arhyme many of us may have innocently repeated in our childhood illustrates the theme of this chapter. Gender can be seen as a subject of complexity that elicits great emotion and affects all of us daily, influencing the way we dress and behave. Much has been written and many civil battles fought on gender issues and rights. In the early 21st century, UK legislation seems to be moving towards equal opportunities for all. How much further it should proceed is a question that makes gender issues so controversial. But what might these issues mean for parents of young children? This chapter reports parental attitudes and children's experiences of gender roles in relation to toy play in their homes.

There were two main reasons for this study: first my personal work experiences and interests as an early years teacher; and second the specific Armed Forces environment in which the study took place. The overall aim was to investigate the research question:

What is the impact of gender on parents' attitudes and children's experiences of play with toys in the home?

I began by looking in detail at more general gender issues and at how children develop their own gender identity.

Methodology

The study considered parents' views and children's experiences. So it was important to choose the right methods of data collection for both groups of participants. I decided to carry out interviews with parents as the major research method because this would allow me to develop and clarify issues raised by the parents. The interviews generated a rich variety of data for, as Patton (1982) suggests:

> We interview people to find out from them those things that we cannot directly observe... we cannot observe feelings, thought and intentions.. we can't observe how people have organised the world and the meanings they attach to what goes on in the world – we have to ask people questions about those things. (p161)

The first part of the study investigated parents' feelings, thoughts and intentions concerning gender issues and toy play. The planned interviews allowed me to gain knowledge and information about each person's values, preferences, attitudes and beliefs. I gave considerable thought to the format and structure of the interviews and the type of interview that would best suit this study.

Interviewing parents

Choosing the right kind of interview was, I felt, the key to a successful study. The range of alternatives could be plotted somewhere on a continuum of formality, from formally structured and under the full control of the interviewer to less formal, more open interviews which adopt the style of a conversation – the interviewer allowing the interviewee to direct the focus and flow. In the latter, a social relationship may develop between the participants. In the first extreme, the aim is to eliminate bias, gain 'reliable' data and strive for research credibility of the type which seeks to emulate a scientific experiment. The opposite extreme resembles fictional storytelling: it seeks to find out the individual's perspectives on the world, their assumptions, experiences and feelings. It is not verifiable 'truth' that is being sought here but personal perspectives, such is the theory of method, but in reality one interview may span a mixture of genres and they are rarely situated at either end of a 'continuum of formality'.

The format of the interviews with parents included a variety of open and closed questions, designed to elicit rich responses from parents about their attitudes towards gender roles and their children's toys. This type of interview could be located in the middle of the 'continuum of formality', striking the balance between direct questioning on the topic and probing into issues the parents raised during the interview.

I also wanted to use the best methods for gaining insight into the children's home experiences, so I asked each set of parents who agreed to be interviewed to complete a two-week 'play diary', recording what toys their children played with at home.

> In many instances, diaries are advocated as a means of gaining access to situations in which it would not normally be possible to obtain data. (Burgess, 1994 p310)

Gaining access to all the homes to observe the children individually would have been time-consuming and intrusive, and my presence as an observer (and their nursery teacher) would probably have influenced the children's behaviour. Parents were in a better position to record their child's play habits over a longer period, with less likelihood of distortion or interference.

The difficulties of using diaries include the time involved and the possible effects of the observer on the behaviour. I devised a two-week 'play diary', with space for parents to indicate which toys their child played with, to whom they belonged and where and how the children played. I hoped to use the data to learn something about the parents' attitudes and identify any similarities and differences between families and between the mothers' and fathers' views. I also wanted to understand the experiences of the children so that I could compare parents' attitudes and the children's experiences.

The sample

I chose a small sample of the population on the military base in which I worked, and issued an open invitation to the parents of the children in the class of four-year-olds in the nursery serving the military families posted abroad. The first five parents of girls and the first five parents of boys who offered to be involved were invited to take part.

Thirteen adults were interviewed: five mothers of girls, five mothers of boys, one father of a girl and two fathers of boys. All were aged between 30 and 40 years and their occupations are listed in Table 1.

Table 1 Occupations of mothers and fathers in the sample

Mothers' occupations	Number	Fathers' occupations	Number
nurse	1	Army	8
child care	4	Navy	1
beauty therapist	1	RAF	1
translator	1		
no paid work	3		

During the time it took for volunteers to come forward, I piloted the interview with another similar group of military families. The piloting exercise proved invaluable, highlighting the questions that needed to be amended and any issues that needed further consideration.

Ethical issues

In any form of research it is important to consider ethical guidelines or protocols. My study involved many people directly so I needed to pay close attention to the process of data collection, analysis and dissemination. As Blaxter *et al* (1996) indicate:

> Research ethics is about being clear about the nature of the agreement you have entered into with your research subjects or contacts... and is about keeping to such agreements when they have been reached. (p 141)

I was careful to ensure confidentiality to the parents and to explain how I would use the data they supplied. The intimate nature of the interview ruled out the possibility that it be anonymous, but all data were subsequently anonymised and treated with confidentiality. All the adult volunteers were eager to participate and agreed to talk with their own children about keeping a 'play diary' and ask them if they had any objections to doing so. Respecting every research participant as an individual was an important moral issue highlighted in the pilot for the study. It is necessary to take into consideration any personal worries, nervousness and show each person due respect. They should not leave the experience with any sense of failure or loss of self-esteem (Cohen *et al.*, 2000).

Bias is another ethical dilemma in any research process. When interviews form the major source of data the issue of bias is particularly poignant. The interpersonal relationship that may develop between researcher and participant could influence the data collected. A rich and varied amount of data can be collected through interview and the challenge is to report the findings faithfully. The skill of the researcher lies in uncovering the 'truths' sought to fulfil the objectives of the study. It is not enough merely to report the spoken word; such nuances as hesitation and demeanour may also be informative and must be noted.

Every research project has to consider ethical issues, and in my study I drew up a personal code of ethical practice concerning my obligations to the research participants and also issues of informed consent and confidentiality. The research methods I chose could be prone to bias and open to interpretation so these issues also needed consideration.

Some key findings
The parents in the ten families were aged between 30 and 40 years, all the fathers worked in the armed forces, and four of the ten mothers worked in childcare. Some research issues arising from this study may directly reflect their daily work, knowledge and experiences and thus, their responses to interview questions may differ from those of families with no military connection.

The fact that the play diaries were all completed by mothers was interesting in itself. Were mothers more involved in playing with and providing toys for their preschool children? It would have been fascinating to have been able to compare diaries completed by fathers. The difficulties of involving fathers in research are not specific to this study; Beal (1994) comments briefly that 'mothers are more often available to participate in research projects than fathers' (p19).

The aim of the research project was initially to investigate gender roles and toy play at home and to understand the effects of adult attitudes to gender roles on children's play with toys. One of the research aims was to look in depth at parental contributions to their children's experiences of toy play at home. The study indicates contrasts between adult male and female gender attitudes towards play in the home. Such gender bias was identified from interviews and revealed a clear trend towards the fathers' gender views as rigidly stereotyped and the mothers' as less rigidly expressed. The gender assumptions indicated by parents in this study reflect examples from previously documented research such as Beal's (1994). Beal's data also highlighted fathers who had set ideas of what toys they perceive appropriate for boys and girls to play with, whereas mothers made fewer distinctions between girls' and boys' toys.

Throughout my study it became apparent that parents had different expectations for young boys and girls. The adults involved generally accepted that girls can play with a wider variety of toys than boys. The fathers' prejudice against boys playing with 'girlie' toys was evident and the initial display of tolerance towards equality of toy play shown by mothers was marred by their concerns about what other people might think.

The mothers' responses indicated that they were well aware of the gender discrimination that took place. However, 'being aware of discriminatory behaviour is not enough. It requires action' (Bruce, 1997 p186). Action taken to redress stereotypical views or gender specific toy play in their home was not an issue recounted in the interviews, but it is nevertheless an issue of consequence. In terms of preschool practice, to be aware of such discriminary behaviour can be seen as a key step in affecting policy and practice in an early years setting. It may not be enough, in educational settings, for children simply to have equal *access* to toys deemed appropriate for one gender or another. If there is a balance that needs to be redressed, a decision must be made as to whether play between girls and boys needs to be actively encouraged and, in addition, the value of actively encouraging children of both sexes to play with toys hitherto associated only with one.

Reasons for buying toys

Mothers and fathers offered similar reasons for buying toys:

- a special occasion (birthdays, Christmas and Easter)
- when visitors came to stay
- as treats or rewards for good behaviour
- for an educational purpose.

Table 2 Mothers' and fathers' suggestions for appropriate toys for girls and boys.

Mothers' suggestions of suitable toys for boys	Mothers' suggestions of suitable toys for girls	Fathers' suggestions of suitable toys for boys	Fathers' suggestions of suitable toys for girls
Lego	dolls (general)	Lego	dolls
jigsaws	dolls' house	cars	cuddly toys
footballs	Barbie and accessories	guns	books
Play Mobile	cuddly toys	footballs	
books	art/craft equipment		
scooters	balls		
trucks	dressing up clothes		
Bob the Builder toys	jewellery		
cars, fire engines, diggers, forklifts	Lego		
	books		

Who chose the toys	For Boys	For Girls
mother	1	3
father	4	1
both parents	1	4
grand parents	2	2
other relatives	1	1
friends	2	2
child	5	2

Table 3: Who chooses toys for the children?

Parents also mentioned safety, price and influences on children's choice (such as advertising, television, films/videos).

Naming a favourite toy

The majority of parents found it difficult to name just one favourite toy but they said that their boys' favourite toys included construction and cars or trucks. For girls they nominated soft toys, Barbie dolls and dressing-up clothes. Table 2 shows mothers' and fathers' suggestions for appropriate toys for girls and boys, and Table 3 indicates who chooses the toys bought for the girls and boys in the survey.

Toys parents do not like their children to play with

One mother said that guns should not be seen as a plaything:

> *Every time we go in or out of camp you see the soldiers on the gate with guns. That's where they should stay. I tell my children that they are for Daddy's work, to help him stop any bad people, they are not to play with.*

The issue of guns was brought up by three other mothers, though one said that play guns or water pistols were fine, as they were, 'only pretend'. Two mothers suggested that they could not stop their child from playing with pretend guns, as they saw someone carrying a gun everyday. One father was passionate about this issue; he was the father of a boy in the study. He believed that it was fine for his son to play with a water pistol, but was resolute that he could not and should not be dressed in any form of uniform or camouflage. When asked to expand on this point, he answered tersely, 'I don't think it's right, he is not old enough for that'.

A further major topic raised concerned 'fads and trends' in children's toys. The participants used these words to describe toys that move in and out of fashion very quickly, such as Pokémon and Digimon toys. Seven of the thirteen parents interviewed made comments about these, all indicating that they would not buy a toy just because it happened to be this year's trend. The general feeling was that these particular toys were a waste of money, as they were not played with very often and soon replaced in the child's favour by another toy. Concerns were expressed that Pokémon characters and their merchandise were a cause for arguments or fights at home as well as at school, and parents tried, with some difficulty, to avoid them. They blamed the media in general and, specifically, a local producer of crisps who put a Pokémon card in each packet. They recounted stories of their children being in tears if the card was lost or not the character they needed to extend their collection.

Parents views on gender-appropriate toys

The parents were asked whether they thought any toys were more appropriate for boys or girls to play with. Books, jigsaws and favourite cuddly toys were suggested by twelve out of thirteen parents as 'non-sexist' toys. The father's opinions were concise, indicating that girls could play with most kinds of toys, whereas they would not like to see boys playing with make-up, dressing-up clothes or 'girl's dolls'. They offered the suggestion that it was more acceptable for girls to be seen playing with cars than it was for boys to play with a doll. One father was taken aback by a photograph of his son helping a friend dress a large baby doll in the home corner at nursery and commented, 'He does not play with any dolls at home, he has never been interested.'

The mothers' comments were more extensive than those of the fathers but dolls and doll play seemed to generate much thought for all parents. Nine of the ten mothers talked about the different types of dolls available and the children's preferences. They suggested that girls liked baby dolls, which they could feed and dress, and boys like Action Man to play 'rough and tumble with'. Two mothers said that at this early age, children did not mind which toys they played with, and that they thought that availability and accessibility of the toy influenced the child's choice. Three other mothers talked about their own children playing happily with their sibling's toys, even when the sibling was of a different age and gender. A brother and sister played happily side by side with a Barbie and an Action man, both using the dolls' house as the focus of play. One mother regretted that her sons did not have the opportunity to play freely with 'girls' toys at home, as her brother had. She said that she did not buy any 'girls' toys for her boys because of the additional expense and their father's disapproval. She remarked that 'the youngest one gets a chance to play freely at school, which is good.'

Three other mothers indicated that gender distinctions were now old fashioned, remarking, 'Well, both men and women share the house work these days' and, 'Most women have a career too, although some of us have to put it on hold out here'; and 'Boys and girls are treated more equally now'. Two mothers discussed wider issues of gender. One talked of society's views concerning young boys being dressed in pink, or expectations for mothers to dress baby girls and boys in different coloured outfits. Another focused on the environment in which she was living. The questions she raised involved the effects on her daughter of seeing her dad as the main breadwinner in the family, about the 'imbalances of mums and dads going out to work' and about her own career that she had to 'put on hold to come out here with my family'. This mother wanted her daughter to be able to choose whatever career she wanted. Although fathers seemed to see gender typing of toys in a narrow frame, the mothers' opinions were less confined. The mothers raised many issues that influenced children's ideas and opinions, including peer pressure, the environment and their husband's views.

Children's experiences as recorded in the two-week play diaries

The play diaries indicated the toy choices children made at home. Each parent chose a specific time each day to observe their child at play and noted the types of toys. Table 4 summarises what the children played with at home.

Types of toys	Number of boys who played with these	Number of girls who played with these
soft toys	0	4
construction	5	2
dolls/accessories	3	4
natural items (shells, sticks, sand, water)	4	5
Art/craft equipment	1	3
dressing up clothes	1	1
bikes/trikes	4	4
books	1	2
computer/game boy	3	1
balls	2	1
cars/vehicles	2	0

Table 4: Children's choices of toys at home

Socialisation of play

The most popular outside play environment was the beach and the most popular indoor environment was the front room/lounge. During the two weeks, the children played alone and with others. Table 5 shows how may times over a period of fourteen days each child was observed in lone play or play with someone else and also lists their favourite toys as observed at home and nominated by the children themselves.

Each completed play diary contained adjectives describing the children at play. The words used to illustrate the girls at play were, in order of frequency: quietly, with concentration, co-operatively, engrossed, with imagination, sensibly, nicely, inventively, noisily, argumentatively. The words on the boys' play diaries were, again in order of frequency: noisily, roughly, energetically, with frustration, with distractions, argumentatively, annoyingly, engrossed, quietly.

Table 5 Summary of play diaries of play alone and with others and details of favourite toys

Individual children	Playing on their own	Playing with someone	Favourite toy (as observed at home)	Favourite toy (as stated by the child at nursery)
girl 1	5	9	Barbie	dolls
girl 2	7	7	Barbie	Dancing Barbie
girl 3	6	8	bike	dressing up clothes
girl 4	5	9	art/drawing	teddy and dolls
girl 5	7	7	dolls	cuddly duck
girls average	6	8		
boy 1	3	11	bike	new bike
boy 2	1	13	computer	game boy
boy 3	2	12	natural items	action man
boy 4	5	9	cars	car and fire engine
boy 5	4	10	football	car and trucks
boys average	3	11		

Types of toys played with

The list of toys generated by parents (see table 2) contrasts with the list of toys highlighted by the play diaries (see table 5). None of the parents mentioned computers or computer games, although four of the ten children were seen playing with them during the two weeks. Bikes were not listed by parents but both boys and girls were observed playing on them. The popular toy of the moment, Pokémon, though a concern of parents, was absent from any diary. The only toy mentioned in the diaries that has earned 'trend' status was Barbie.

Barbie, in her many guises, together with her products, was very popular with all five girls in the study. This doll regularly centred in four out of the five girls' play sessions. The issue of doll play was another that highlighted differences between children's experiences and parental views. Three of the five boys were recorded playing with dolls during the two weeks. One diary entry was accompanied with three explanation marks. This diary related to the young boy whose father did not like the idea of him playing with 'girls' dolls'. The notes indicated that during the two weeks, play involved his sister's dolls house, pram and Barbie dolls. The first diary entry was the one with the multiple explanation marks and recorded the boy playing with his Action Man in the dolls' house. Two of the other boys' diaries mentioned doll play; in both cases the parent specified what type of doll. The majority of cases noted that the boys played with their own action dolls, but in five recorded instances the boys were playing with their sisters' or friends' baby doll or Barbie.

Parents' suggestions about toys for boys and girls were different and the views of mothers and fathers were also contrasting. The three fathers offered a simple and, arguably, stereotypical view of which toys were played with by boys or girls. The mothers' views were less fixed, offering more suggestions of toys they deemed appropriate for each sex. This is in keeping with recent studies on the topic.

> It seems that fathers play an especially important role in signalling the types of play that children should avoid. (Beal, 1994, p8)

The three fathers in this study expressed set ideas of what was appropriate for each sex. Mothers did not voice such clear boundaries.

Only a few toy items appeared in both the boys' and girls' lists of toys. Balls figured but footballs were specified in the boys' list, and no such specifications on the girls' list. The play diaries bore out some of the parents' perceived gender distinctions. No boys were observed playing with soft toys and no girls with cars. Both sexes were involved in dressing-up games but here parents offered clarification: a boy was noted to have dressed up as a soldier and a cowboy, and a girl as a 'princess in all her frills'. Detailed explanations were also made when diary entries recorded boys playing with dolls. The doll was named in each case, for example: Action Man and a description of the play was added, for example: 'Roughly, the doll was sliding down the roof of the dolls' house and knocking out the furniture.' The use of multiple explanation marks in another boy's play diary, when a dolls' house was mentioned, also seems to reveal the parents' views on this issue.

During the research, it became apparent that the gender of siblings influenced the choice of toys in the family. Interviews and diary evidence both suggested that children who had siblings of the opposite gender played with a wider variety of toys. The ways toys were played with was also influenced, but to a lesser extent. After observing classroom role-play, Paley (1994) makes relevant suggestions about brothers and sisters learning how to play from each other.

> Unless you are playing with your little brother at home, bad characters need reinforcements. The boys have been teaching this lesson to girls for years. (Paley, 1994 p99)

It was the mothers in the study who commented on the change they perceived in play actions if siblings were present.

> It has been argued that family configuration of siblings influences mothers' expectations of their male and female children. (Yelland, 1998, p43)

This idea is supported by views recorded from the mothers in this study. Six parents made specific comments on the issue of siblings. Two briefly mentioned siblings sharing most toys and playing happily together. They inferred that a girl calmed her brother's play. In contrast, an older brother was said to have introduced cars into his sister's play. Three others talked in more detail about specific cases where a child was playing with their sibling's toys, remarking that if the siblings were of the same sex, some types of toys would not be available. The sixth parent gave a complex explanation of how her two boys and one girl showed differing interests in the home-made dolls' house. Age was the influential factor, in her view. The inference was that when all her children were young, they had loved the dolls' house, whereas the oldest boy had now lost interest. The parent's reasoning was that his age, and the expectations put upon him by his family, peers, and society had affected his choice. Christensen and James (2000) support this notion by stating that

> Not only do family members of different ages have diverse functions, but they also receive unequal rewards. (Christensen and James, 2000, p45).

The use of natural items as playthings was another significant factor in the children's play diaries. There was no mention of such items in any of the interviews. However, all but one child was seen to be playing with sand, water, sticks or shells. The climate, time of year, and geographical features of the environment may have influenced this choice of play item. Many children were frequently recorded in their diaries as playing on the beach.

Children's favourite toys

Parents were hesitant to identify a favourite toy for their child but still distinguished between the choices of boys and girls. The standard suggestions were that boys like cars, trucks and construction toys in contrast to the soft toys, Barbie and dressing up games that the girls seem to prefer. The trend reinforced other evidence gained during the research process. For example, from the list of toys generated from the play diaries, girls in this study appear to favour doll play, with boys having a more varied selection of toys but with a focus mainly on construction and transport. The trend leans towards a stereotypical view of girls' and boys' toys. If children are experiencing these stereotypical divisions in toy choice, the implications is that there will be wider developmental considerations in relation to gender.

Where the children played

Girls and boys both played indoors and out. The uniqueness of the environment itself may be accredited to having influenced the choices of where children played, including the proximity of numerous beaches to the participants' houses and the constant high temperatures. The relative safety offered by the enclosed military campus may also have been an influential factor.

Further avenues of study

This study, with its rich and varied data, could well stimulate further enquiry. For example; given the frequent mention of doll play in both the interviews and play diaries, a deeper understanding of parents' views on young boys' play with dolls would be interesting. Of course, the doll play of some boys with the military association of Action Man figures looks quite different from girls' doll play with Barbie and other fashion dolls. Further work could invite fuller participation by the children. The children in this study were not directly involved and opportunities remain to understand something of children's own views of toys, their gender identity and ideas of self and others in relation to gender.

Lindon notes that adult attitudes and views are important in helping to shape children's development:

> Children need and deserve a sense of self-esteem, and pride in their own sources of personal identity...Children can learn prejudiced views and a conviction of their own superiority. They are not born feeling and believing that some other people are less worthy than themselves. However, offensive and arrogant attitudes learned by some children will become stronger, unless responsible adults work to counteract the views of any actual misinformation. (Lindon, 1998 p5).

However, adults do not stand alone in their position of influence; a child's gender identity is influenced by many other factors – biological, cultural and social. Toy play has been observed in this small-scale study as one area in which children do differentiate between the sexes, with adult participants having varying but notable effect on, and control of, their experiences. The influence of siblings and peer groups on a child's gender identity was a fascinating aspect of the study and one that could stimulate further work. Age too was a factor; parents saw gender as a greater issue in how and what children played with as they got older.

This study took place in a military environment and, without comparative data, it is difficult to ascertain the impact of this on the outcomes. Finally, this report should include some consideration of rights and equality. All children are different and these differences should be acknowledged as a means of recognising and nurturing individuality. As Nutbrown (1996) states: 'Every child should have the right to feel good about themselves' (p24).

As an early years practitioner one is in an ideal position to help young children realise this right. To create a sensitive ethos in a setting is vital. As Lloyd (1987) demonstrates, children as young as thirteen months can be influenced by gender bias, but in supportive nonbiased settings these children will have the opportunity to develop into confident young people, secure in themselves and tolerant of others, male or female.

References

Beal, C.R. (1994) *Boys and Girls: The Development of Gender Roles* USA: McGraw-Hill

Blaxter, L. Hughes, C. and Tight, M. (1996) *How to research* Buckingham: Open University Press

Bruce, T. (1997) *Early Childhood Education* London: Hodder and Stoughton

Burgess, R.G. (1994) On diaries and diary keeping. In Bennett, T (1994) *Improving educational management through research and consultancy* London: Paul Chapman Publishing

Christensen, P. and James, A. (2000) *Research with Children: perspectives and practices* London: Falmer Press

Cohen, L. Manion, L. and Morrison, K. (2000) *Research Methods in Education* (5th Edition) London: RoutledgeFalmer

Lindon, J. (1998) *Equal Opportunities in Practice* London: Hodder Headline

Lloyd, B (1987) Social representations of gender In J. Bruner, and H. Haster (eds) *Making Sense: The Child's Construction of the World* London: Routledge

Nutbrown, C (1996) *Respectful Educators – Capable Learners: Children's Rights in Early Education* London: Paul Chapman Publishing

Paley, V.G. (1994) *The Boy who was a Helicopter* Cambridge Mass.:Harvard University Press

Patton, M.Q. (1982) *Practical Evaluation* USA: Sage

Yelland, N. (ed) (1998) *Gender in Early Childhood* London: Routledge

11

Dolls with stories to tell: understanding bias and diversity

Gill Farmer

This chapter was written following the terrorist attacks on the World Trade Centre in New York and the Pentagon in Washington when the world entered a period of uncertainty. Reprisals were taken against Muslim communities in Britain and America soon after. During the continuing conflict in the Middle East and 'the war against terrorism' children have continued to pick up messages about attitudes and behaviour. A child's environment and the people in it play a crucial formative role in developing a child's attitudes to other individuals, their family, community and the wider world.

The philosophy of the schoolroom in one generation will be the philosophy of government in the next. (Abraham Lincoln)

Dolls with a story to tell

The dolls that provoked the interest for this study are called Anti-Bias Persona Dolls, based on the work in California of Kay Taus and the Anti-Bias Task Force (Derman-Sparks, 1989). The physical and visual presence of a Persona Doll greatly intensifies the involvement of children with a story. The individual identities for the dolls are created to reflect the physical characteristics, background, lifestyles and circumstances of children. Many things are communicated to us through stories. Good stories capture children's hearts, minds and imaginations; they are a useful way to communicate values and positive messages (Taus, 2000).

Telling stories is an ancient and beautiful art. The tellers of stories, the transmitters of legend and history, the weavers of Celtic folklore, Germanic myth, Asian wonder tales and Dreamtime stories are part of a tradition going back into the annals of time. There is a power in story telling; the teller is free to watch the audience, to lead or follow every changing mood, free to use eyes, voice, body, as aids in expression; the words too are of the moment, spontaneous and only for one audience. Children generally listen more eagerly to a story told than to one read; the listener gets the story plus the enthusiasm of the storyteller. A well-told story captures the imagination, speaks to the heart and communicates in a powerful way to children.

Through stories young children can learn about situations, people and lifestyles that are different from their own. Children can start to see the world through other people's eyes. Stories can change the way children perceive the world, how they react and respond to it. The use of dolls, each one with a life story of its own, offers young children the opportunity to explore issues of social justice. The dolls help adults and children explore the four objectives of the anti-bias approach. Firstly, by reflecting lifestyle differences so that each child can feel good about who they are. Secondly, by exposing children to human diversity so that each child can feel comfortable with dif-

Figure I

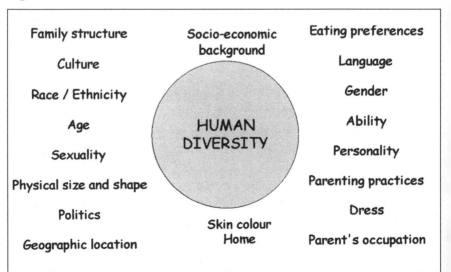

ference in others. Thirdly, to stimulate discussion, explore empathy, stereotypes and critical thinking so that each child can identify bias and stereotypes and the hurt they cause. Finally by providing stories that encourage children to stand up for themselves and others against prejudiced attitudes and behaviour (Derman-Sparks, 1989).

Giving a doll an appropriate persona involves careful and respectful selection of characteristics to represent a fictitious child's life. Figure 1 (adapted from Jones and Mules, 1997 p8) identifies aspects of human diversity that could be introduced.

Louise Derman-Sparks (1989) suggests that the stories emerge from four sources: children's daily lives, current world events, history and information that the practitioner wants children to have. Stories about the doll are always told by the adult; the doll does not speak or answer questions. The dolls are a focus for the children, to give a story meaning. By simply telling the story the adult allows the discussion and problem solving to be child-directed. Difference is something that children and adults should feel good about. Difference should not be an excuse for stereotyping, bias, exclusion or discrimination. By identifying and empathising with the dolls, children are helped to see injustice in the stories, take on the role of problem-solver and look for a solution. The dolls are usually the size of a two-year-old; hand made or bought, cloth or plastic and dressed appropriately. Each doll represents a real person and maintains its own identity. Kay Taus (1987) suggests that the dolls be kept in an accessible, special place, visible and available for play but only if 'you ask first'.

The Project
The intention to introduce Persona Dolls into the lives of students was sparked by attendance at a conference reporting on the first phase of 'Persona Dolls: education without prejudice'. Funded by the European Commission's Socrates/Comenius programme, co-ordinated by the Early Years Trainers Anti-Racist Network (EYTARN), the project involved partners from Britain, Denmark and the Netherlands. The display by the British partner comprised thirty-inch dolls, each with a persona, created by childcare and education students. A second conference in November 2000 allowed for a reassessment of my intentions to introduce Persona Dolls to

first year BTEC Early Years students studying Values and Personal Development. Glenda MacNaughton, the guest speaker at both conferences, stimulated and inspired but was also the catalyst for some rethinking. At the second conference the huge responsibility on the storyteller became evident. The content must be accurate, well researched and positively presented. It appeared frighteningly easy to offer inappropriate messages that reinforce stereotypes rather than challenge them.

My work with the students had already raised concerns about some of their own attitudes. It could be argued that the attitudes of the students aged 17-50 involved with this inquiry were already formed. By early adulthood individuals have developed attitudes about other people and the groups to which they belong. Attitudes are made up from feelings influenced by personal experience, with an added intellectual element that is formed by expectations, assumptions and beliefs (Lindon, 1998 p11). Attitudes cannot be seen, but they emerge through actions and words. Erikson, Kohlberg and Piaget offer hypotheses about the construct of identity and morality. Chris Gaine (1995) precisely summarises the dilemma:

> The point that I am making is that these 18 and 19 year olds have for the most part grown up in the home counties, in towns like Worthing, Winchester and Bexhill on Sea, and they write what they have heard. They write the expressions, ideas and stereotypes that have surrounded them all their lives, spelling out the constructions of Black and Asian people which have been available to them. How much they believe them, resist them, or combat them is a different question; our problem is that in the 1990s these attitudes still reflect the climate in which they have grown up. (Gaine, 1995 p3)

It became apparent that it would not be viable to replicate the thirty-inch Persona Dolls nor to put their substitutes into work placements. Suitable dolls about nine inches high with soft bodies were found, that were comfortable to hold, came in four skin tones and with no facial features and were affordable. Each student would be involved in telling their doll's story to their peer group.

Methodology

Using action research as my methodological framework, the study looked at the effectiveness of using Persona Dolls to develop understanding and tolerance with two groups of students working towards a BTEC National qualification in Early Years. The introduction of new units into the course framework presented an opportunity to investigate how students would approach issues of diversity and tolerance, using a teaching and learning project that combined story-telling and equality and equity issues.

The design of the study fits into the spiral of action research. Kemmis and McTaggart (1992) see action research as a collaborative collecting of evidence based on group reflection and questioning motivated by the wish to improve understanding to effect change.

> *Action research is concerned equally with changing individuals, on the one hand, and, on the other the culture of groups, institutions and societies to which they belong. The culture of a group can be defined in terms of the characteristic substance and forms of language and discourses, activities and practices, and social relationships and organisation which constitute the interactions of the group.* (Kemmis and McTaggart 1992 p16)

Research methods and data collection
Students needed to complete the assignment in order to achieve the required learning outcomes for the Values and Personal Development unit. The data created comprised: the eleven dolls and their personal stories, 25 personal logbooks recording critical incidents, with a written evaluation based upon their individual entries. In addition students took part in focus group interviews.

Persona Dolls
A Persona Doll was created, its features and clothes added and its personality and background constructed. Students worked together in pairs or small groups to research and gather background information for presenting an authentic story.

Student log books
'Critical Incidents' are stories used as tools for conducting research on oneself. Newman (1987, 1991) suggests that critical incidents can arise through reading, overhearing a conversation or suddenly noticing how someone else is doing something you've always taken for granted. Latent critical incidents are everywhere and they offer important opportunities for examining personal beliefs and learning about professional practice. Students were asked to record critical incidents in their personal logbooks: factors in their personal life, the

media, verbal or non-verbal reactions they had witnessed, read or heard that related to diversity and tolerance. As each represented one person's viewpoint, these accounts could be perceived as purely subjective. McNiff *et al.* (1996 p19) contend, 'It could be that they have been produced more systematically and with less bias than the more 'objective' accounts'. Each student recorded any relevant incidents, conversations or comments in an exercise book to use for this individual part of the assignment.

Focus Group interview
Focus group interviews use a structured process with unstructured content. They are particularly useful for exploring and contrasting attitudes and experiences, appropriate for gaining a broad overview of a particular subject and for presenting and generating new ideas. Kitzinger (1994, 1995) argues that interaction is the crucial feature of focus groups; it enables participants to question each other, reconsider and re-evaluate their own experiences and understanding. Krueger (1994) summarises a focus group as:

> A carefully planned discussion designed to obtain perceptions on a defined area of interest in a permissive non-threatening environment. The discussion is often enjoyable for participants as they share their ideas and perceptions. Group members influence each other by responding to ideas and comments in the discussion. (Krueger, 1994 p6)

The focus group was small but the participants were forthcoming, honest and open. The questions followed Krueger's (1998) framework for focus group interviews comprising opening, introductory, transition and key questions. Open-ended questions were used; asking 'why' and giving examples was avoided. Participants were asked to 'think back' and in conclusion offer ideas for future considerations.

Ethics
Kantian moral philosophy, which guides much of the writing on research ethics, allows that individuals must be respected and cannot be used as a means to an end. The British Educational Research Association (BERA) believes that gaining ethical clearance for a research project involving people should not be an optional process,

> *All educational research should be conducted within an ethic of respect for persons, respect for knowledge, respect for democratic values and respect for quality of education research.* (BERA, 1992 p1)

For the purposes of this study full information about the purpose and use of the participant's contributions was given to both the students and the institution. I have tried to ensure anonymity by changing all names.

Interpretation of the data

How students responded to a challenge never fails to amaze me. I had no preconceived ideas about how this project would evolve and develop. I did have apprehensions about the logbook and how it would be perceived. I was concerned that the participants might not be prepared to write their honest reflections, thoughts and ideas or that they would write what they thought I wanted to read. The results connect carefully created dolls and their stories with relevant entries from logbooks. The contents were informative, rewarding, unexpected.

The dolls and their stories range across culture, creed and ability. Molly and Tracey tell a straightforward story about Emily. Emily's new spectacles are the focus for empathy in her story. Initial reactions to the assignment led me to consider that Molly and Tracey felt uncomfortable with the idea of addressing more explicit issues of discrimination. In her logbook Molly considers the plight of asylum seekers and reacts to her aunt's disparaging remarks: 'She was cross that I did not agree with her. She said I do not have to live with them. I backed down to avoid an argument.' Molly records several personal incidents including one when she was in the car with her son and when she called the driver of the car in front 'Grandad', she suddenly saw how children learn stereotypes.

> A said 'Is that Grandad's car?'
> I replied, 'He is someone's Grandad, but not yours'
> A said, 'Why did you call him Grandad then'
> I replied, 'Because he is going so slow, and all Grandads go slow'
> A said, 'What, even my Grandad?'
> I answered, 'Yes'. This was a very unfair comment – but one I often use. I was frustrated at the driver and now A thinks that Grandads are all slow.

DOLL	PERSONA	ASPECT OF DIVERSITY
JUREMA	Creators: Louisa, Sally and Ruth. Jurema is English, 3½ years old, youngest of three. Mother, a doctor is from Angola. Father a 'house husband'. Holiday - a first visit to Angola. Doll has two outfits, for England and for Africa.	Story tells of different climate, food, clothes and traditions. "Two days after their Carnival they take food to the beach and place it in the sea as an offering to the mermaids. The food that is offered is sweet cone, made from beans, vegetables and pork".
MAYRA	Creators: Nina and Judy. Mayra is Thai, with an English mother, Thai father, 3 years old, with an older and a younger brother. The family has recently arrived from Thailand. Mayra likes painting, poetry, stories and playing with dolls.	Finds speaking English difficult and is very shy at nursery. Mum is a vet. Dad cooks Mayra's favourite food – rice and fish. Dad a doctor is studying for a year in England after which the family will return to Thailand.
ROSA-MAY	Creators: Ellen, Mary and Anna. Rosa-May is English, 5 years old. Mum a nurse, Dad a fire fighter, two brothers. Rosa–May soon to start school with her friend Amy. She enjoys swimming, horse riding and loves animals.	At 2 years old Rosa May contracted meningitis and as a result has complete hearing loss. Starting in mainstream school, communication is only through sign language. Works with a speech and language therapist.
SANTINIA	Creators: Jan and Diane. Santinia is 7 years old, English, and her parents are Spanish. They live with her grandparents and travel as a group of six caravans. Liti her rag doll is carried in a bag. She enjoys drawing and painting, as she has no television in the caravan.	Romany travellers who live in a caravan pulled by horses. The family travels for 6 months and return to village life from autumn to spring. They all wear traditional clothes for festivals and special occasions like the two-day "Homage to Sara the Black".

Figure 2

Name of doll	Family structure.	Occupation classification. (NS –SEC)		Housing
Ayisha	Nuclear, 3 children	Accountant and teacher	1.2	House
Emily	Nuclear, 2 children	Previously farming	4.	4 bedroom large house
Emma	Nuclear, 3 children	Not stated		3 bedroom bungalow
Jurema	Nuclear, 3 children	Doctor and house husband	1.2	4 bedroom detached
Josh	Nuclear, 3 children	International company - no level		Nice house near beach
Kim	Nuclear, 2 children	Not stated		House
Laura	Nuclear, 2 children	Both parents work in the media	2	Large semi-detached
Mayra	Nuclear, 3 children	Doctor and Vet.	1.2	Not stated
Rosa-May	Nuclear, 3 children	Nurse and fire-fighter	2 2	Not stated
Santinia	Extended + 1 child	Not sated		Caravan / cottage
Sita	Nuclear, 3 children	Not stated		Not stated

(NS – SEC) National Statistics Socio-economic Classifications (Rose 2001)

Figure 3

As I compiled the photograph table [Figure 2] I became aware of several interesting aspects of the persona stories. The table of family structure and lifestyles of the Persona Dolls [Figure 3] reveals some conspicuous similarities.

All but one of the dolls come from nuclear families; only Santinia lives with grandparents and is an only child. The parents whose occupations are recorded all work in respected jobs or professions; their housing reflects high-income levels. Knowing the individual students I am amazed that there is no mention of single parent or re-constituted families, no attempt to address issues of sexual orientation or gender stereotyping. Where it is mentioned, living accommodation is spacious, except in the caravan. Activities like ballet, horse riding, reading and swimming dominate. None of the dolls live in flats, small terraced houses, bed and breakfast accommodation, tithe cottages or on an estate. It appeared that many of the students created stories with elements of the lifestylcs they aspire to or felt comfortable relating.

I confess to wondering why Jurema, Mayra and Laura are all of mixed race, and whether the Celtic or Anglo genealogy factor made the doll or the story more acceptable. 'Laura is English of Welsh parents and her father is of West African parents who are naturalised'. Laura's story centres on her cerebral palsy. Kathryn and Nancy who created Laura describe her as a 'privileged child'. Her parents work in the media, her grandparents, from the Gambia and Wales, are from professional backgrounds and live close to the large semi-detached family home in a leafy suburb of a large southern town. The focus on Laura's cerebral palsy allowed Kathryn to become involved, as extracts from her logbook reveal.

10th April

I have had the persona doll in the back of my car since the end of term. Each time I get in I have seen the doll lying there and have had a feeling of discomfort about it. I think the thing is that I wish I had picked up a white doll. I just don't feel happy talking in front of a group of adults about something that is not a subject that I feel qualified to talk about. I'm worried that in making the doll and discussing this with the class I will end up giving a more stereotypical and unhelpful picture of what it means to be black than if I just kept quiet ... I am confident that I would be able to discuss issues of race with children without coming against these problems, but I just don't feel comfortable with the way we are doing it.

28th April

Amy is a three-year-old girl I have been working with who has mild cerebral palsy. This has affected her ability to walk so that she has needed a lot of support and help with this, which is why I was going to her nursery with her to give her more confidence.

13th May

> *I made some clothes for the persona doll last night, and for some reason I am feeling better about it all. Nancy and I have talked about ideas for her character, and I feel the whole thing seems a bit more possible than it did before.*

Anna used her logbook quite differently:

> *I found this whole assignment very thought provoking. Writing the logbook was for me quite a painful experience as it made me look back over very sad and difficult times. ... In the end I decided that it was important that this little boy's story was told because I know this experience has changed my whole life.*

Anna recounts Ben's story. Ben is profoundly disabled and has lived with Anna and her family for 5½ years. He arrived at her foster home weighing eleven pounds at just over a year old. 'When he came to me I had never in my life met a disabled person before'. The narrative described the life, death and everyday struggles Ben and the family have faced in those five and a half 'precious years'. Anna depicts discrimination from differing viewpoints; her own for some of the professionals she deals with, having to 'thank at least five people to gain entry to the simplest of places', and putting up with people who stare and point. 'In my local supermarket the manager stepped back into a display of toilet rolls because she was staring so hard at us'.

Several students, including Alex and Nina recorded their reactions to an advert on Southern FM, which announced to prospective customers that: 'polite, happy to serve, giving you a smile – that's not what you expect from a teenage shop assistant'. Both resented the stereotype – as Nina said 'We are all 16-20 and we are encouraged to smile and go the extra mile.'

Students considered issues of tolerance related to individual children, items from the media, the news, their work placement and their work with the dolls. Some entries in the logbooks show that little opportunity for equality or equity has reached certain of the children:

> *This evening I worked at a home for children with special needs. I was shocked at the way the adults took care of the kids. It was as though they didn't think the children were human.* (Alex 10th May 2001)

We have a new Portuguese girl at nursery. She can speak in English but hasn't yet. One of the staff said to her 'Oh come on! Stop being stubborn and playing around.' But she is probably still very nervous, I certainly would be if I didn't know the language very well. (Diane 4th May 2001)

I was talking to the manger (who knows Amy well) about possibly working with a boy upstairs. Amy [with Cerebral Palsy] was with me, and was listening to our conversation. At one point the manager described the boy as having 'learning difficulties like Amy'. I was shocked that Amy could have been at the nursery all this time and the manager could have come to understand so little about her. (Kathryn 28th April 2001)

Some students avoided confronting or responding to uncomfortable issues of tolerance of diversity in their logbooks. One student failed to address any issues of diversity in her entries. Several focused exclusively on ability issues; many ignored the racial tension widely reported in the media. Some students were able to address issues of their own. Because her grandfather was Romany, Diane was interested in the research to add to her 'family history'. Not all her results were positive, however.

Today someone in our group was asking what persona our doll had. When she found out she typically stereotyped and made remarks. Due to the fact that my Grandad was a true Romany I took offence at this. (Diane 22nd May 2001)

During the focus group interview Mary recalled her reaction to the Romany doll:

That was the only doll that made me think of something. I didn't really think any more about them but I had to put, did put thoughts into my logbook. That doll, it addressed a prejudice I had, whereas none of the others did.

In her logbook Mary recalled an incident from her own childhood prompted by one of the group commenting, as if mimicking a child, 'my daddy says gypsies leave rubbish'.

Instantly I thought yes and they steal. I presume this is a generalisation, I do not know any Travellers. Two girls from a

*permanent gypsy camp used to come to my parties when I was
at primary school. They were my friends and were welcomed
into my home. Although my mother admitted the other day that
she had hated them coming and would try to persuade me to
invite someone else.*

*Looking back over this I see that my mother has had a great
influence on my views. I am perhaps quick to judge people if I
do not know the reasons for their actions and I need to put myself in their position and look at things more objectively before
forming an opinion.*

Just creating the Persona Dolls would not have given the students insight into what they themselves understood about diversity, tolerance
or themselves. The logbook was an essential component of the
assignment and the research.

Personal understanding

Everybody has the capacity to change but some people die before they do.
(Louise Derman-Sparks)

I have no doubt about the power of Persona Dolls and their stories.
The work of Kay Taus (1987) Tricia Whitney (1999), Glenda
MacNaughton, (2000a, 2000b) and Babette Brown (2001) has
identified opportunities for children and adults to investigate the
social world around them, using a variety of Persona Dolls to help
children to encourage and console one another and to address issues
of bias, diversity and equity.

*Above all we have learnt that the Persona Dolls and their stories are a powerful
tool for practicing anti-bias work with children. They excite children's interest,
they fascinate adults and intrigue parents. This interest, fascination and intrigue
provokes conversation, and encourages exploration of what children know, how
they know it and how we might help them construct fair and equitable meanings about themselves and others.* (MacNaughton, 2000b p12)

The education and care of children from a wide range of backgrounds, cultures, family structures and lifestyles is taking place in
a variety of settings. It is becoming increasingly important that the
care and learning environment must reflect each child's life, family
and community, whilst providing every child with the skills to grow
up and live in our diverse society. Young children do notice differences and they experience bias in their own lives.

Enabling children to think critically and speak up when they believe something is unfair will empower them and allow their participation in what Paulo Friere calls:

> The practice of freedom; the means by which men and women deal critically and creatively with reality and discover how to participate in the transformation of their world. (Friere, 1972 p15)

Before we can help children to develop these skills we must first learn them for ourselves. The main focus of research and literature relating to Persona Dolls concerns the interaction between children and dolls. Babette Brown (2001 p155) refers to the dolls that initiated this project and the positive effect on the students involved. Unfortunately she does not report how information about students' attitudes was gathered and evaluated. My early concerns that the students might inadvertently offer mixed or negative messages to children were unintentionally corroborated in some of the logbook entries:

> I decided on a career in child care because I felt issues of inequality are best addressed from a young age. However, although I can see the very positive use persona dolls can be put to I worry that in unskilled hands they could have the opposite effect. (Nancy, June 2001)

> I think the concept of the persona doll is very powerful and the person using it needs to be very confident as no one can be totally prepared for the questions children might ask. Without being melodramatic the answers given to children may affect their thinking for the rest of their lives. (Anna, June 2001)

In challenging the 'truths' of class, age, status, race, ethnicity, gender, ability or language superiority, I intended the students to develop understanding and tolerance for diversity. I would not presume to suggest that their attitudes, long-held prejudices or assumptions have been altered by the project. But from the content of the logbooks it is possible to identify that 21 of the 25 students were able to relate to at least one area of diversity, address their own concerns and show awareness of how intolerance, discrimination and prejudice affects everyone.

For the future

There are only two lasting bequests that we can give our children. One is roots, the other wings. (Hodding Carter Jnr.)

In Australia and the United States Persona Dolls are widely used. Many of the proponents are involved with educating and training teachers and child care practitioners. There is a profusion of descriptions about introductory workshops, the enthusiasm of participants and their ensuing involvement (Carter, 2000; Colunga, 2000; Jones and Mules, 1997). No mention is made about the attitudes of practitioners. The participants who go on to introduce and use Persona Dolls seem to be self-selecting, dedicated to the anti-bias curriculum, and they find stories to be an ideal way to raise important issues on racism and cultural diversity.

It would seem that there is an opportunity for further work by educators in the post-compulsory education and training sector, to investigate attitude change and identify effective methods for on-going anti-discriminatory training. Life-long learning applies to everyone working to combat discrimination. An evening meeting, a one day in-service seminar, even a short course will not be enough. At the end of a 15-week Racism and Human Development course a postgraduate student reflected:

> Tonight was our last class. I've been thinking about why it affects people so much. I think it's because, in untying the knot, you're unravelling the web of lies that each of us has inevitably experienced, and racism is only a part of the false information each of us received while growing up. Racism is the part that is the most blatant. There are many parts that have taken their dehumanising toll, and in unravelling even a bit of the whole, we feel tremendously excited. We have only to unravel more of it to reclaim ourselves completely. (Derman-Sparks and Brunson-Phillips, 1997 p137)

Practitioners and children applying the skills learnt through an anti-discriminatory, anti-bias approach to education and life promote a culture of tolerance and a celebration of the diversity within our society. It would be wonderful if all children could learn in such an environment.

In linking the research to Persona Dolls this inquiry adds to a body of theory. Its approach to developing understanding about tolerance and diversity appears to be unique. The major theories of human development can be used to support or refute the findings.

Adolescent and young adult students experimented with the roles of creator, storyteller and observer (Erikson, 1959, 1968). Piaget and Kohlberg agreed that moral reasoning required both a certain level of cognitive development and life experiences (Jarvis with Chandler, 2001). Information from this research identifies individuals who have looked, revisited and evaluated their attitudes. Erikson (in Santrock, 1994) determines that in middle adulthood our chief concern is to assist the younger generation in leading and developing useful lives. Without constant reflexivity, evaluation of knowledge and attitudes, each stage of human development can be reinforced by stereotypes, prejudice and discrimination. The findings seem to support Chris Gaine's assertion that those of us working 'in towns like Worthing, Winchester and Bexhill on Sea' still have a huge amount of work to do.

References

British Educational Research Association (1992) *Ethical Guidelines*. (ONLINE – http://www.bera.ac.uk/guidelines.html)

Brown, B. (2001) *Combating Discrimination Persona Dolls in Action*. Stoke on Trent: Trentham Books

Carter, M. (2000) *Uses of Persona Dolls*. (ONLINE – http://www.teleport.com/~people/margiec.html)

Colunga, C. (2000) *City of Phoenix Head Start Persona Doll Project* (ONLINE – http://www.teleport.com/~people/phoenix.html)

Derman-Sparks, L. and the ABC Task Force (1989) *Anti-Bias Curriculum: tools for empowering young children* Washington DC: National Association for the Education of Young Children

Derman-Sparks, L. and Brunson-Phillips, C. (1997) *Teaching and Learning Anti-Racism: a developmental approach* New York: Teachers College Press

Erikson, E. (1959) *Identity and the Life Cycle* New York: Norton

Erikson, E. (1968) *Identity and Youth Crisis* New York: Norton

Friere, P. (1972) *Pedagogy of the Oppressed* New York: The Seabury Press

Gaine, C. (1995) *Still No Problem Here* Stoke on Trent: Trentham Books

Jarvis, M. with Chandler, E. (2001) *Angles on Child Psychology* Cheltenham: Nelson Thornes

Jones, K and Mules, R. (1997) *Persona Dolls Anti-bias in Action* Sydney, Australia: Lady Gowrie Children Centre

Kemmis, S. and McTaggart, R. (eds.) (1992) *The Action Research Planner (3rd edition)* Geelong, Victoria: Deakin University Press

Kitzinger. J. (1994) 'The methodology of focus groups: the importance of interaction between research participants' *Sociology of Health* 16 (1) pp103-121.

Kitzinger. J. (1995) 'Introducing focus groups', *British Medical Journal* 311 pp299-302

Krueger, R. (1994) *Focus Groups: A Practical Guide for Applied Research (2nd edition)* Thousand Oaks CA: Sage

Krueger, R. (1998) *Developing Questions for Focus Groups* Thousand Oaks, CA.:Sage

Lindon, J. (1998) *Equal Opportunities in Practice* London: Hodder and Stoughton

MacNaughton, G. (2000a) *Rethinking Gender in Early Childhood Education*. London: Paul Chapman Publishing

MacNaughton, G. (2000b) *Dolls for equity: young children learning respect and unlearning unfairness* Victoria Australia: Department of Learning and Education Development University of Melbourne

McNiff, J., Lomax, P. and Whitehead, J. (1996) *You and Your Action Research Project* London: Routledge Falmer.

Newman, J. (1987) 'Learning to teach by uncovering our assumptions', (ONLINE – http://www.behs.cchs.usyd.edu.au/arow/reader/newman.htm.) *Language Arts*, 64(7), pp727-737

Newman, J. (1991) *Interwoven Conversations: Learning and Teaching through Critical Reflection* Toronto: OISE Press.

Santrock, J. (1994) *Child Development. (6th edition)* Dubuque, Iowa: WCB Brown and Benchmark

Taus, K. (1987) 'Teachers as storytellers for justice'. Unpublished master's thesis, Pasadena, CA : Pacific Oaks College

Taus K. (2000) The Powers of Persona Dolls (ONLINE – http://www.teleport.com/~people/persona_dolls.html)

Whitney, T. (1999) *Kids Like Us. Using Persona Dolls in the Classroom* St. Paul, MN.:Redleaf Press

12

Does inclusion work? Simon's story

Tracey Ann Berry

Introduction

This chapter explores the factors that appear to promote or inhibit inclusion from the perspectives of four children educated in both mainstream and special schools, their parents and teachers. Practical issues and the attitudes of those who have been through the inclusion process form the main focus of the chapter.

Purpose of the study

Inclusion is currently a high profile topic of debate amongst politicians, teachers and other professional educators. The number of children 'included' in mainstream schools is rising rapidly, but so too is the number of exclusions. This chapter offers an insight into what inclusion feels like for those who are included and asks: 'does inclusion work?'

Personal views and values are developed and evolve through individual experiences and so life experiences may change perspectives (Perera, 2001). The UK Government and its policy makers do not necessarily see at first hand the practical effect of policy changes in the classroom or understand the impact of different policies on each other. Some educational policies arguably challenge the drive towards inclusion (see Nutbrown, 1998 for example).

This chapter reports the findings of four case studies; two children who had recently entered mainstream schooling after beginning their education in a special school and two who had recently transferred from a mainstream school to a special school because inclusion had not worked for them. The children were all boys, aged between 6 and 7 years at the time of their moves and all had 'moderate learning difficulties' and 'minor behavioural problems'. Each child had a statement of Special Educational Needs.

Historical overview
A brief history of inclusion
In the UK at the start of the 21st Century the increasing demand for inclusive practices and educational opportunities for all children appear to contradict and be in competition with policies focused on raising academic standards and achievements. There have been many policy struggles throughout the history of the special education system in England and Wales, which need to be explored in the wider socio-economic context.

Special Education has existed in different forms for many years so practices may have changed. In the mid 19th Century the 'new' Industrial Age saw disabled people as a threat to social order and they were therefore institutionalised and 'treated'. Under capitalism, the unemployed, poor and disabled people were confined and forced to labour to maintain their upkeep. Later in the 19th Century people were separated into different categories depending on how useful to society they were judged to be. They were then divided into specific 'defective' groups and sent to various institutions. Following the 1886 Idiots Act those classified as 'idiots' were sent to hospitals or institutions. 'Imbeciles' were identified as a separate group, less defective than idiots, and yet another group emerged who were classed as 'feeble-minded' children. The 1899 Elementary Education (Defective and Epileptic Children) Act formally introduced special education for those children termed feeble-minded, as it was recognised that these children posed an economic and educational problem to the Government.

The growth of a separate system of education for disabled children coincided with the Government becoming the main educational provider in England. However, the development of special schools was underpinned by many different factors. Due to the introduction of compulsory elementary schooling, many children who were previously excluded appeared in the education system; consequently a number of children were seen not to achieve the required standards. Schools were held accountable and those categorised as 'failing' lost funding. The outcome of compulsory schooling was not an acceptance of diversity but exclusion of those children who did not meet standards (Pijl *et al.*, 1999).

Clough (2000) identifies five different perspectives on educational inclusion that give a certain picture of the historical development of ideas and practice: the psycho-medical legacy; the sociological response; curricular approaches; school improvement strategies; and disability studies critique. Though each perspective inevitably overlaps with the next and the five at times occupy the same ground with different – and sometimes competing – emphases and popularity, Clough's diagram below maps the historical territory of the five eras leading towards inclusion.

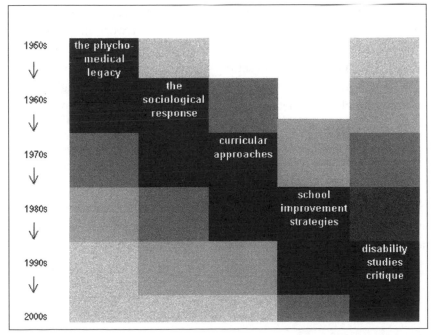

(Clough, 2000 p9)

(Reproduced by kind permission of the author and Sage Publications)

Methods and methodological issues for the study

A case study approach was taken in order to provide a fuller picture of the individuals in relation to their environment. The children were all observed in their new school settings to see how they were coping in their new environments. Interviews were undertaken with the children, their teachers from current and previous schools, and the four sets of parents in order to gather information about the build-up to a change of school, the effect of 'inclusion' on the children and family, issues raised by teachers and to obtain opinions on possible future improvements that could be made both within the individual schools and within the education system as a whole.

Listening to the voices

The voices of the participants in my study needed to be presented in their original context. They allow us some insight to the thoughts and findings of the children, parents and teachers. As Peters points out 'capability for change ultimately rests with the authentic voices of people with disabilities' (Peters, 1995, p73).

As a Special Needs teacher I have seen inclusion take place and have often initiated the inclusion process, but I do not work in a mainstream setting so have never included a child with Special Educational Needs in a mainstream setting. Consequently it was important that I listen to the real experts – those who have lived through the process of inclusion whether successful or not. However, I recognise that

> Researchers have to listen very carefully to 'voices from inside', but in conducting their research they should operate as independent outsiders. (Pijl, et al, 1999, p26).

Space in this chapter is too limited to present all the cases involved in this study but *Simon's story,* followed by my interpretation of the lessons to be drawn from his story, is given here in full.

SIMON'S STORY: from exclusion in mainstream to an inclusive community in a Special School

Simon's perspective

On his old 'mainstream' school

I don't like it ..... Well, I liked playing football but the work was too hard. I got into trouble and it made Dad shout and it made Mum cry ... My sister still goes there and she likes it. It was boring a lot cos I had nothing to do when everyone else was working, but I liked playing with Karen. Karen didn't come all of the time though. She was my friend.

On his new special school

It is loads of fun. I play football every week and sometimes I win. Claire lets me play on her computer too. The work is okay and Maureen or Paula or Jenny always help me with my work.

Simon's mother's perspective

On contact between schools before transfer

As far as I am aware not a lot because it was my decision to take him out, which we did fairly quickly. As far as I am aware there was literally just a file handed over. I don't know what conversations took place. He had his auxiliary come with him for a couple of weeks but, from what I was told from her, there was not much going on. Nobody was interested in what she was doing there. It was all sort of 'he is going now, we don't want to know.'

On her involvement in the transition process

I initiated it so I was fully informed. I had to do something because he was getting nowhere ... The last report we received was 100% negative and I am glad he has moved.

On staff at this previous school

The Reception teacher was supportive in a way but it was not within the teachers' capabilities to do things about it because the Head did not want to know. He did not access anything. Money was there waiting to be applied for. The Head tried to tell me there were no funds available. The Authority had the funds but the Head did not access them. He told me they had no Special Needs children in his school. I know for a fact that he would certainly have children on the Special Needs Register. I could identify them in the playground. It was like banging your head against a brick wall with him. He just would not listen.

On contact between schools after transfer

I am not aware of any contact. I just remember hearing a sigh when he left. I would be very surprised if they did ever make contact. They are just not interested.

On problems in the previous school

The staff did not understand him at all and he was left alone with just a voluntary helper each afternoon not doing any work. He was really unhappy and the Head did not want to know. His old school worked for some, it was not going to work for him. They were not going to make any concessions for him or children like him. It is sad for Special Needs kids who are going to go there. If they had wanted they could have used Simon as an example of how they were going to do things. There are Simons everywhere. They could have had a little unit or some specialist group there for kids like Simon.

On problems in the new school

Initially he picked up some terrible language – he had come from such a structured school, a very high-class neighbourhood and was suddenly thrust into a completely different environment.

On progress in the new school

I think he is doing very well. He is happier in himself; he has certainly just started doing things, started reading things.

On her own views on inclusion

Simon has been categorised as having Attention Deficit Hyperactivity Disorder but I think it is more than that. There are so many aspects to him and I think he is definitely on the Autistic Spectrum. He needs a school that understands him and works with him, rather than trying to change him. Inclusion can be good and it can be bad. It is a necessary evil probably. It is lovely to keep them protected in a special school. It doesn't do them any good in the long run. They need to be integrated at some point. It is finding the right point. It is definitely finding the right point and doing it for the right reasons. You cannot just plonk them in the catchment area school. They have got to go to the right place for the right reasons, not because it is their time to go, but because they are ready to go – at whatever stage, at whatever point. Mainstream inclusion has got to be good but it has got to be individual and not just across the board. Individual needs need to be looked at.

Simon's Mainstream Teacher's Perspective

On Simon

Simon had a lot of difficulty sitting in a class/group situation. He would make strange noises. He was not able to interact when a story was discussed. He needs to be on a one-to-one basis. He could at times, without meaning to be, be aggressive with the other children. He wasn't vicious at all – he could be quite boisterous. We very much felt that he needed an environment where he had more opportunity to have large play – to be able to let go of his energy a little bit more than he was able to in Reception Class. These were the main difficulties really – that he was not able to interact in a whole class or group situation. He needed one-to-one all the time really.

On classroom management

Simon didn't get his support until the end of the Reception Year. Luckily I had two Classroom Assistants for the first term. In the second term I only had help in the afternoons so the mornings were quite difficult. He did improve as the year went on and, while I took a full class lesson, he was able to do a jigsaw or occupy himself reasonably well. In the afternoon he very much got one-to-one with the Classroom Assistant

On the factors that led to Simon leaving

I really felt we didn't have the right equipment for him. In my opinion he needed a lot of games and hands-on things. He couldn't discuss things like the rest of the children could. He needed to have hands on all the time. I felt he needed large play as well, which we didn't really have. He did come into PE but I felt that he really could have done with climbing frames and things like that, which we just didn't have. I felt he needed a lot smaller groups than we had. He didn't cope in the class really well – we had about 25 in the class. Even within a small group within that class he still couldn't particularly cope because he was not working at the same level as the rest of the children academically either, as well as his behaviour.

On changes that could have enabled Simon to stay in mainstream school

Some large play equipment and some more specialised equipment – special needs equipment, would have helped him as well. He did have some games that he could use but we didn't have enough variety to keep him interested and occupied. Plus, I felt that I didn't have the specialist knowledge that I needed to be able to work with Simon effectively. The Classroom Assistants that worked with him were excellent with him, but I didn't feel that I knew enough about the problems that Simon had to be able to help him properly. I did what I could for him but I would have liked a bit more knowledge about how to go about helping him more than I did.

We got a little bit of external advice but to begin with, it was just 'he is just a naughty boy, you have got to keep him down' and 'it is just a language problem, talk to him a lot.' Then a psychologist came out and came up with a very, very good report for him but nothing practical came from that, other than what we did ourselves – finding out what did and didn't work. Basically we needed help and we got it, mainly from teachers at the special school.

On her own views on inclusion

I found that the rest of my class suffered that year. I had to spend a lot of time with him. The class had to put up with interruptions all the time – shouting out – noises. They had to put up with physical abuse sometimes. Physical is the wrong word – Simon would hit out without knowing he was doing it. There was one parent who complained about that and wanted him moved. I felt the rest of the class did suffer in terms of that and needing more of my attention. The Classroom Assistant was meant to be for the whole class and a lot of the time she was with just Simon. I think, for the rest of the class, inclusion can have a detrimental effect on them.

I don't want to say that I want children to be segregated or taken away because they are different – that is not how it is, but when you look at it practically, I don't feel I had the resources, nor had the pupil: teacher ratio or the knowledge. If I had those, if I had Classroom Assistants, if I had access to all the equipment and had plenty of knowledge of how to deal with him, and I could be sure that a child with special needs being there was not going to affect the rest of the children, I would have had no problem with it. I found it interesting. In some ways it did benefit the rest of the class because, socially, they were very good with him. They accepted him, they helped him and they were smashing with him. Generally they didn't leave him out, so I saw that as a positive effect of having him there. There were just so many other disadvantages on the other side really, which is why I thought he would be better somewhere else.

Conclusion: lessons from Simon

Inclusion is a very complex process. As Barton and Corbett (1993) point out, changes in the education system need to be both conceptual and structural. It will not work if children are simply pushed into schools which are already pressurised to meet targets. As Slee (1993) highlights, inclusive education

...necessitates a reconsideration of the complex and potent cocktail of pedagogy, curriculum, school organisation and the ideologies that inform these components of schooling. (p351)

Teachers' views are crucial in regard to inclusive practices (Fulcher, 1989). The teacher is one of the most important determinants of whether inclusion will be successful or not, and where inclusion does not happen it is because people with the power to accomplish it don't want children with special needs or disabilities in mainstream schools (Booth, 1983). However, the structural constraints that teachers have to deal with must be recognised and for inclusion to work all teachers need to have core information about Special Educational Needs, have the necessary knowledge and skills and a positive attitude towards the education of these children (Mittler, 1993).

This small-scale study highlights the fact that some teachers feel that they just do not have the training or the resources to deal with children with SEN. In which case it is unfair to both the child and the teacher to place children in mainstream schools and expect everyone simply to manage. This clearly did not work in Simon's case. My own belief is that he should have stayed in the mainstream school as he needed to develop his social learning; his behaviour was not especially challenging and academically he required only minor adaptations to the curriculum. In fact, when he first entered the special school he was working with a group of children who were in the process of being included into mainstream schools. However, Simon's mainstream teacher felt she had inadequate training to cope and little support within the school. Under those circumstances Simon needed a change of placement, as inclusion of any type will only be successful if all parties are committed to it; otherwise children with SEN in mainstream settings are, ironically, excluded from their classmates and general social and learning experiences.

The policy conflicts of the late 1990s and early 2000s, and the drive for a competitive educational system, mean that there is still no national commitment to respond to the needs of *all* children. In the current system teachers fully committed to inclusive education can find themselves compromised by the pressures of trying to raise standards, meet academic targets and properly include children with learning difficulties.

If we return to the original question which drove this study: *'Does inclusion work?'* the answer would clearly be 'yes' in some cases and 'no' in others. Inclusion is not possible for every child in the present educational, political and social climate. Many disabled children are presently better placed in provision where staff are highly trained – and properly supported – to meet their needs. Full inclusion is the ideal, but this will take time. Success or failure for four children with moderate learning difficulties in this study depended upon how effective mainstream schools were in integrating differences. Success hinged, too, on teacher attitudes. Teachers in mainstream settings need critically to reflect on their practices and the values they are passing to *all* children. Achievements are unimportant if they are not viewed in the context of school communities that improve and enhance the spirit of teachers and learners (Fielding, 1999).

Good quality, qualified support for children with SEN is often difficult to find. Learning support for children was a concern of every parent in my study, regardless of whether or not inclusion was successful. An influx of, mainly untrained, Classroom Assistants has been brought into the education system to work with some of our most needy children. When this support is taken away, often due to funding issues, 'teachers feel that they can no longer cope' (Ainscow, 2000, p105).

We need to tackle this issue – unqualified, inexperienced staff can hinder the whole inclusive process. Many, many changes are needed if schools that were designed to suit only selected pupils are to change so that they can meet the diverse needs of all children. Priorities include:

- further training for *all* teachers

- training and funding for qualified Support Assistants

- improved collaboration between various professionals and between teachers and parents

- closer relationships between special and mainstream schools to share good practice

- the sharing of expertise by teachers within schools.

There is a rich resource of people skilled and committed to an inclusive education system. The question is how to realise inclusion in practice. After five decades of development through the psycho-medical legacy, the sociological response, curricular approaches, school improvement strategies and disability studies critique (Clough, 2000), we might ask what phase will come after inclusion. As we look to the future with hope, we could ask if the next movement towards inclusion will be described as 'equity'.

References

Ainscow, M (ed) (2000) *Effective Schools for All* London: David Fulton.

Booth, T. (1983) Policies towards the integration of mentally handicapped children in education *Oxford Review of Education*, Vol 9, No 39, p255-68

Clough, P (2000) Routes to Inclusion In Clough, P and Corbett, J (eds), *Theories of Inclusive Education* London: Paul Chapman Publishing, p 3-33.

Fielding, M (1999) 'Communities of Learners', in O'Hagan, R (ed) *Modern Educational Myths*, London: Kogan Page

Fulcher, G. (1989) *Disabling Policies? A comparative approach to education policy and disability* London: Falmer Press

Mittler, P. (1993) Preparing all initial teacher training students to teach children with Special Needs: a case study from England. *European Journal of Special Needs*, Vol 7, No 6, p 417-439.

Nutbrown, C (1998) *Baseline Assessment and Baseline Assessment for Special Educational Needs: differences and difficulties* London: BAECE Early Education

Perera, S. (2001) Living with Special Educational Needs: mothers' perspectives In Clough, P and Nutbrown C. (eds) (2001) *Voices of Arabia: Essays in Educational Research* Sheffield: University of Sheffield School of Education

Peters, S (1995) Disability Baggage: changing the education research terrain In Clough, P and Barton L (eds), *Making Difficulties, Research and the Construction of Special Educational Needs*, London: Paul Chapman.

Pijl, Y J, Pijl S J and Van der Bos K P (1999) Teachers' motives for referring students to Special Education In Ballard, K (ed), *Inclusive Education : International Voices on Disability and Justice*, p10-27.

Slee, R (1993), The politics of integration – new sites for old practices? *Disability, Handicap and Society*, 8(4), p351-360

13

Managing challenging behaviour: positive approaches

Ramona P. Khan

Force and fear have no place in education.
(Albert Einstein)

Introduction

This chapter discusses the factors which influence the effective use of positive approaches to managing young children's behaviour, in the twin islands Republic of Trinidad and Tobago – a culture where corporal punishment remains legal (Trinidad and Tobago, 1980). The practices of one early childhood educator (who grew up in this society) and who successfully implements alternative methods in managing young children's behaviour are presented and reflected upon in the light of recent literature. The chapter considers: the laws and policies that govern behaviour management by educators in the islands; the effects of physical chastisement of children; the benefits of alternative methods of managing behaviour; the importance of training for early childhood educators.

Reasons for challenging behaviour

Behaviour management is one of the major challenges facing educators today across the world. In Trinidad and Tobago specifically, educators in early years settings have been reporting increased aggression and indiscipline in young children and there have been calls for a different, less punitive, approach (Mandol, 1998; Rostant, 1999).

Family life

Many factors contribute to unacceptable behaviour but the lack of secure family environments and the demise of the extended family in Trinidad and Tobago is a major contributor to children's difficulties (Curwin and Mendler, 1988).

Violent societies

Young children today are exposed to images and experiences of violence; in their everyday lives, at school, at home, in the community, through the media, violent cartoons and 'war' toys. Pre-school children can also be influenced by violence on television (Carlsson-Paige and Levin, 1992), and because very young children are affected by violence, awareness of how to address violence in young children's lives is critical for early childhood professionals (Levin, 1994; Riak, 1992; Slaby *et al.*, 1995).

The rod and the law

The 'rod', inherited from the British system during colonial times, still features in schooling in Trinidad and Tobago and corporal punishment is a culturally accepted method of managing children's behaviour in schools (Sylvester, 1995). The laws governing the management of children's behaviour in Trinidad and Tobago seem silent on the issue of corporal punishment in the school system because the ordinances that specifically stated how corporal punishment should be administered were repealed in 1966 and no replacements were entered. However, according to common law Section 22 of the Trinidad and Tobago Children's Act, teachers do have the power to administer 'reasonable punishment' which includes corporal punishment (Trinidad and Tobago Ministry of Education, 1980).

In 1990 The United Nations General Assembly unanimously adopted the Convention on the Rights of the Child and in 1991 Trinidad and Tobago ratified this international treaty. Fifty-four Articles assert the rights of children but Article 37 pertains directly to punishment and states that:

> No child shall be subjected to torture or other cruel, inhuman or degrading treatment or punishment. (UN Convention on the Rights of the Child 1989 Article 37)

Changing services and society

While deans, educators and principals have been administrating corporal punishment, early childhood educators at Servol (*Service Volunteered for All*) a Non-Governmental Organisation in Trinidad and Tobago, formulated a policy almost thirty years ago that no form of physical punishment would be used at any of their preschool programs. *Servol's* work began with displaced adolescents who did not pass the qualifying examination for admission to high schools. The founder of *Servol*, Fr. J. Pantin, a Roman Catholic priest, saw that many of the problems plaguing the youths stemmed from their negative early experiences and so he embarked upon establishing early childhood education provision in depressed communities in Trinidad. Many children in these *Servol* Early Childhood programs came from families in difficulty, where there was much domestic violence. Non-violent methods were therefore crucial in managing the children's behaviour and so a programme of training for the early childhood educators began.

Training Early Childhood Educators

The adult training programme has now been running for over 20 years and follows the principals of androgogy. The needs of these trainees differ tremendously as does the experience they bring to the learning milieu. *Servol* recognises these needs and attempts to cater for them through programmes which are built on the principle of self-directed adult learning. In Trinidad schooling is still didactic and teacher-directed, students assuming the role of passive recipient. The experience that *Servol* trainees bring to the learning arena is rich and varied and the experiential approach to training values in a number of ways, by: utilising personal experience; selecting materials learners can relate to; drawing on a range of instructional media such as discussions, drama, classroom-based experience, case studies and simulations.

At *Servol* alternatives to smacking and beating children have always been a part of the teacher training program. It is during this training process that the punitive philosophy is examined and alternative methods studied. Alternative methods for behaviour management are based not only upon an understanding of child development but also on age appropriate curricula. Developmentally appropriate practices (Bredekamp, 1987) and expectations are the foundations upon which the management of children's behaviour is studied.

Punishment

Teachers have many reasons for punishing children. Most common is the lack of a role model, and so adults who have not had role models who could communicate strong emotions such as anger and frustration in a constructive way and respond to children who are 'out of control' by taking over control instead of helping the children to learn self-control. Physical punishment is often an indicator that the adult has had no training in alternative methods. Many teachers are afraid that if they do not respond to the child's offending behaviour firmly enough the child may be tempted to repeat it (Curwin and Medler, 1988).

Punishment, an action deliberately chosen to cause suffering in order to teach a child a lesson (Kohn, 1996) may be physical (corporal) and/or psychological. Such punishments include suspension (out of group, class or school), detention (extra work or lines), humiliation, often in front of peers (criticising, blaming and shaming) and withdrawal of privileges or involvement in activities. Punishments such as these do not help young children to remember how to behave appropriately – they just make children suffer. So when young children are punished they remember the fear or resentment created by the adult's anger. They may retain the message that they are 'bad' or 'naughty' but not necessarily understand the reasons for the anger or how they themselves might do things differently. Even if a child realises that certain behaviour is unacceptable, the punishment may not change their behaviour in the long term (De Vries and Zan, 1994).

Punishment only changes behaviour temporarily, if at all, so maintaining the new behaviour requires sustaining a punitive system in which punishment, or at least the threat of it, is repeated over and over. Such systems are popular in some societies and regimes around the world because punishment and rewards appear to work, at least in the short run. Children are easily manipulated by promises, treats, loss of privileges, threats or possible isolation in a time-out area. These systems do little to help children learn how to express needs and feelings or to resolve conflicts appropriately (Faber and Mazlish, 1995). The children cannot internalise the behaviour because they do not make a conscious choice to engage in the behaviour. Punishment by adults deprives children of the opportunity to approach problems constructively and to acquire new social skills. It solves the adult's immediate problem of restoring order. But when adults who teach and care for children use corporal punishment they teach children that hurting others is an acceptable way to achieve order in a group (Slaby *et al.*, 1995).

Positive alternatives to physical punishment

A form of behaviour management that positively affects the lives of children is *Servol's* alternative to physical punishment. This incorporates strategies for developing a philosophy about behaviour management based on an understanding of child development which includes physical, social, emotional and cognitive needs. *Servol's* approach requires educators to hold realistic expectations and an awareness of a child's dignity and self-esteem (Faber and Mazlish, 1995). Kohn (1996) proposes that educators should reflect on the needs of children and how these can be met, rather than concentrating on coercing children to do what is expected of them, and it is this which is the main focus of the rest of this chapter.

Meeting needs – not beating bodies

This section describes some of the approaches of one early childhood educator who – as the following observation shows – had a sensitive awareness of the needs of the children in her group.

Observing Mary with her Kindergarten group

Mary's class has seventeen children, all approximately four years old. As each child enters her class Mary greets them individually with a warm smile and a hug, and asks how they are. The children seem to come bursting with information to share with her. She warmly interacts with the children and responds to their needs for affection and attention, making them feel valued and secure in a non-threatening environment.

During class assembly the children sing songs of their choice and are given the opportunity to share their tales. When more than one child began to speak at the same time Mary quickly asked: 'Do you want to hear what your friends have to say?' Mary appeared to want them to think about her question but not necessarily to answer it, as she then asked: 'How many of us should speak at the same time? Who would like to go first?' One child began, then Mary said ' Okay Brent has decided to speak, everyone will have a turn to share their stories so we can all hear the wonderful things that everyone has to say'.

One morning when the children were still arriving and Mary was organising a large sheet of newsprint, one child asked if she could help. The teacher accepted the offer and while she was chatting with the girl and handing her the pieces of masking tape, a boy came over and asked if he could assist. The girl immediately responded with an emphatic 'no! I'm helping auntie' (as the children call her). The teacher stopped ripping the tape and said 'the more help we have the quicker we can get this done, now one can roll the tape and the other can stick the tape on the paper'. At this response the girl said, ' I'll roll and you can stick Akil'. Almost before she finished the sentence, Akil agreed and beaming with delight, he said 'I'll stick'. The process was well synchronised with great cooperation.

After general assembly the children went to their respective classrooms collecting their chairs from the tables and placing them in a semicircle around the easel. They seemed quite familiar with this routine but there was some crowding. Several children were trying to move through the space at the same time. One little girl asked another to move out of the way so she could pass and the other responded by saying 'I was here first'. On hearing the altercation Mary moved closer to children. The other child waited a moment and allowed her peer to go by. Mary said calmly: 'there is room for everyone, there is no need to rush'.

Free-play time began with a song. Using a chart the children were called to select the area in which they wanted to play. Each learning area facilitates a specific number of participants. This process worked well except for one child who was upset because when it was his turn to choose, the block area was full. Putting her hand on his shoulder, Mary explained that it was full this time, but offered him alternatives of the sand, water or art areas all of which still had spaces available. He hesitated a bit, then made another selection.

The children in this class seemed quite adept at resolving some of their conflicts by talking. Whenever an altercation occurred Mary, who closely supervises the children, positions herself to provide moral support but does not take over the control. Using a constructivist approach, she helps the children to find solutions and offers support as well as encouraging them to think about future situations by asking them what they can do the next time. When one of the children began using physical force to retrieve a block from another child, Jamie asked 'Is there another way to get it back? We need to use our words, not our hands'.

During tidy-up time Mary observed that two girls who had played in the dramatic play area had abdicated their responsibilities to tidy up and returned to their chairs, leaving one child to tidy up the area alone. She went to them, knelt down to make eye contact, and with her arms around both of them she asked them where they had played. When they told her she asked 'and what should you be doing now?' giving them the opportunity – without instructing them – to return and tidy up.

On another occasion one child was heard telling another that she had to get the mop and wipe up the water, because she had poured it on the floor. The child took her peer's direction and proceeded to get the mop. It was evident that the children were already developing some of the social skills they would need in the future.

Reflection on Mary's strategies

Resolving conflicts is an inevitable part of working with young children and this needs to be done in a way which guides children effectively to ensure that difficulties are resolved and harmonious relationships are developed. When children are helped to develop skills they can use in resolving their own conflicts, they develop the confidence to solve problems in their own social realm. The more children try out their skills, and experience success in their relationships with others, the more empowered they will feel (De Vries and Zan, 1994). The role of the educator is crucial in helping children to develop conflict resolution skills (Oken-Wright, 1992). Those who teach young children must support their interactions early on and develop flexible strategies to help young children use language rather than physical force to achieve their goals. Teachers need to keep in mind emotional developmental goals such as independence, competence and autonomy, and act rather than react, intervening and supporting the children's efforts to resolve their conflicts at the right time. Working with young children in this way is challenging and demanding because it is not always easy for young children to think things through before they happen or to consider the points of view of others.

Mary had created a sense of community (Kohn, 1996) in the classroom where children felt respected, trusted and empowered to take some decisions and responsibility. Effective teachers develop specific teaching skills, organise the environment appropriately and prepare thoroughly (Kounin, 1970). Such strategies are important in creating a *positive* classroom and helping to reduce the number of difficulties which arise. When problems do arise they can be used, as Mary did, as opportunities for children to learn more about negotiation, discussion and compromise. Carlsson-Paige and Levin (1992) suggest that children should be involved in various aspects of the decision making process where their ideas are respected. Such opportunities are missed when the adult takes total and immediate decision-making control of the situation or when children are punished. The supportive teacher acknowledges children's feelings sensitively, their ideas are respected and solutions are identified by the children in this process, but it takes time, skill and patience (Oken-Wright, 1992).

As we can see from Mary's practice, alternatives to punishment must include helping children to develop and use *prevention strategies* as well as *interaction strategies* (Faber and Mazlish, 1995). The goal of the process is to help children find and consciously choose alternative, positive ways to express their needs and solve problems. As children solve problems together and engage, by choice, in new ways of interacting they find that successful problem solving has its own rewards.

Conclusions and Recommendations

This final section summarises the factors for success and reflects on the international nature of the issues raised.

Factors for success

Many factors contribute to the successful implementation of positive conflict resolution methods: training; philosophical belief; curriculum; personality; support; and policy. As the work of *Servol* (1992) has demonstrated, *training* is crucial and must include both theory and practice, offering opportunities to observe, discuss and practice – with support – the skills learnt. The development of a *philosophical belief* in alternative methods may arise from training, from personal and political values or both. The effective *curriculum* underpins successful implementation of alternatives strategies for managing behaviour. Child-initiated approaches to learning in an appropriate environment can empower children and help them to feel valued. The *personality* of early childhood educators seems to play an important role in developing a philosophical belief in alternative methods, creating an environment to facilitate implementation of the techniques learnt during training.

Mary is a reflective practitioner, aware of her influence on the development of the young and emotionally vulnerable children in her class. Success requires *support* and where the strategies described in this chapter are successful, the educators do not work in isolation. Supervisory staff, colleagues and the opportunity to continue professional development are all important sources of support. Mary greatly values the continued opportunities for professional development and conversations with colleagues.

Finally, *Servol* put its policy on the management of children's behaviour in place in order to ensure that no child was subjected to physical punishment whilst attending its kindergartens. Clearly stated policies are important to make known, to all involved, the organisation's position. From the policy, training programmes and support mechanisms were developed.

An international concern
Focusing on the physical punishment of children in the Trinidad and Tobago context, this chapter has sought to illustrate and identify alternative methods of managing challenging behaviour in young children. This in a country which – at the time of writing – supports the physical punishment of young children in kindergartens and schools. We need to educate the wider community of Trinidad and Tobago about the negative effects of corporal punishment and the benefits of alternative methods in managing children's behaviour so that we can bring about changes in our cultural practices. Though this study has concentrated on a small twin-island republic in the Caribbean, it is about much more than one small republic or one teacher. It raises issues of international concern. There are many countries and cultures across the world where children are punished because educators – and parents – know no better and where structures do not exist to support them in different practices. There are many countries and cultures too, where, although physical punishment is banned, the positive use of alternative strategies to help children learn to live together in co-operation is not fully exploited.

Educators around the world are faced with many challenges, as we work to provide the best possible learning environments and opportunities for our young students. Education and society, which shape each other, are constantly changing and the reality of these changes suggests that educators everywhere must continually reflect on their practices. As professionals we have a wealth of knowledge from research, beliefs and experience from in and outside the classroom. We must use this knowledge to influence reform, especially when such change will positively affect the children of our society – wherever in the world that society might be located.

References

Bredekamp, S. (1987) *Developmentally Appropriate Practice* New York: National Association for the Education of the Young Child

Carlsson-Paige, N. and Levin, D.E. (1992) Making peace in violent times: a constructivist approach to conflict resolution *Young Children* 48(1), 4-12

Curwin, W. and Mendler, J. (1988) *Discipline with Dignity* Alexandria, Virginia: Association for Curriculum Development.

DeVries, R. and Zan, B. 1994) *Moral Classrooms, Moral Children: creating a constructivist atmosphere in early education* New York: Teacher's College Press

Faber, A. and Mazlish, E. (1995) *How to Talk so Kids will Learn* New York: Rawson Associates

Kohn, A. (1996) *Beyond Discipline: from compliance to community* Alexandria, Virginia: Association for Supervision and Curriculum Development

Kounin, J. (1970) *Discipline and Group Managements in Classrooms* New York: Holt, Rinehart and Winston.

Levin, D. (1994) *Teaching Young Children in Violent Times* Cambridge, MA: Educators for Social Responsibility.

Mandol, N. (1998), Time to banish the Punishment Book, A rest for the rod *Trinidad Guardian* September 8, 1998: p 17 and 25

Rostant, N. (1999) Give respect to get respect from you child *Trinidad Guardian* November 9, 1999 p 16

Oken-Wright, P. (1992) From Tug of War to Let's Make a Deal: the teacher's role *Young Children* 48 (1) p15-20

Riak, J. (1992) *Plain Talk about Spanking* Alamo, CA: Parents and Teachers Against Violence in Education.

Servol News (1992) *Teaching People to Care* Vol. 9, p36

Slaby, R.G., Roedell, W.C., Arezzon, D. and Hendrix, K. (1995) *Early Violence prevention: tools for teachers of young children* Washington D.C.: National Association for the Education of Young Children

Sylvester, M. (1995) We cannot educate without discipline. *The Educational Journal of Trinidad and Tobago*. 13,1 p 11-13.

Trinidad and Tobago Ministry of Education (1980) *The Education Act* Trinidad Government Printery

United Nations (1990) *Convention on the Rights of the Child* UNESCO

Useful Web Sites

Chemelyski, C. (1999) Is Paddling on its Way Back? School Board New (National School Boards) World Corporal Punishment Research Website www.corpun.com

Larzelere, R.E. (1999) Spare the Rod, New Research Challenges Spanking Critics http://www .frc.org/fampol/fpabjpa.html

National Center for the Study of Corporal Punishment, Temple University, Philadelphia. www.stophitting.com/NCACPS/index

The National Coalition to Abolish Corporal Punishment in School

http://www.stophitting.com/NCACPS/index.html

UNESCO Convention on the Rights of the Child

http://www.unicef.org/crc.html

14

Cinderellas in lonely castles? Perspectives of voluntary preschool supervisors in rural communities

Sue Webster

'Gosh, someone interested enough in our plight to study it. Wow!'
(preschool supervisor, 2001)

Introduction

This chapter reports the outcomes of a small-scale study to investigate the perceptions of voluntary preschool practitioners in rural locations. It explores their relationships and experiences within the wider community of early childhood practitioners. The findings have become a tool to evaluate my own practice as a support worker, enabling me to identify ways of raising practitioner motivation, their attendance at training events and their skills in meeting the developmental needs of the children in their preschool settings.

The context of the study

As an outreach worker in a rurally located multi-service early excellence centre, I support and develop voluntary and private early years provision in a market town and its surrounding villages, a geographical area of 320 square miles. This includes 100 practitioners offering places for 720 children from birth to 5 years. Some groups, as members of the Early Years Development and Childcare Partnership (EYDCP), commit themselves to quality standards set by Ofsted and I visit these groups annually for three main reasons: to monitor their progress and offer support to produce and implement post-Ofsted *action plans*; to help to improve practice and to promote involvement in professional development.

The pressure to '*pass*' an Ofsted inspection has, for some less confident practitioners, led to a shift from a play-based approach to the introduction of more formal teaching methods – a problem identified as being detrimental to children's social development (Edwards, 2001). Furthermore the Effective Provision of Preschool Education (EPPE) Project has identified stratification between early years sectors, with some of the weakest outcomes for children in voluntary sector settings, (Sylva, 2000). A play-based curriculum is widely cited as being the most appropriate for children in the foundation stage (Abbott and Moylett, 1999; Nutbrown, 1996; Goleman, 1996). Best practice is most likely to be found in early childhood settings where practitioners are committed, motivated and have a deep knowledge of child development and ongoing access to professional development (Abbott and Pugh, 1998). Nutbrown (1996) asserts that, as knowledge in this field continues to develop, all early childhood practitioners should be 'clear about who they are and their own identity so that they can work together with others to pursue common goals' (p108).

Most of the preschools I support achieve good Ofsted inspection reports but enthusiasm for new developments, initiatives and training participation seems to have declined. A multi-agency approach to early childhood education across England and Wales has its merits but quality is dependent upon equality of opportunity for all stakeholders. Policy makers and managers of national and local initiatives have a duty to address the needs of *all* practitioners, thus requiring a heterogeneous approach, recognising that pay and conditions of employment, support structures, initial education and training and support structures, are often different. These differences can be amplified between different sectors and geographical locations.

Aims of the study and research questions
A key aim of the study was to understand the experiences of the practitioners who participated in the study and, in the wider context, use their practitioner voices to inform and improve practice and policy, (Mills, 1956; Brookfield, 1996).

The research questions I chose to help me fulfil these goals were:

- Do rural preschool supervisors perceive themselves as 'Cinderella' early childhood educators in 'lonely castles', denied the active participation and status afforded to their 'stepsisters' in the maintained and private sectors?

- How does their situation influence their practice?

- What barriers must be overcome to ensure that rurally located preschool supervisors feel that they experience equality of opportunity?

Issues of participation, community agency, professional development and individual needs

Barriers to participation

The 'lonely castle' metaphor suggests the isolation which some early childhood practitioners experience where there are barriers to participation in training or networking, be they situational, institutional or dispositional – or a combination of these factors, – as shown in figure 1, (see Gallagher and Clifford, 2000; McGivney, 1993).

Situational	time, geographical location, costs or work schedules.
Institutional	courses organised to meet the needs of the organisation rather than the student; lack of understanding of the students' needs and their cultural capital – the middle class nature of education.
Dispositional	attitudes, perceptions and expectations of the student
(adapted from McGivney, 1993)	

Figure 1 Barriers to Participation

The barriers for some early childhood educators might well be reduced in a single-sector approach to early childhood education provision but this ignores the secondary benefits of increased parental involvement and the value of a preschools mutuality as community organisations run by the community for the community.

Rural preschools as a community agency

Preschools can offer strong foundations for a community as an agency for financial, human and social capital (Leadbetter, 1999;

Putnam, 2000) and they can widen opportunities for both the children and the adults associated with the group. Many parents who take their children to sessions become involved, attend training and begin new careers as practitioners (McGivney, 1993; Edwards, Siemenski and Zeldin, 1993). As many other rural services have declined in recent years, preschools are often one of the few local services remaining (Williams, 2000). Though often in the minority in a county, rural dwellers nationally constitute 20% of the population (Williams, 2000). Children and practitioners in rural locations have an entitlement to equality of opportunity and their needs should not be neglected because organisation and policy making is made in the interests of the majority urban and city populations (Mills, 1991; Robert, 2000).

Professional Development and Individual Needs
The merits of continuing professional development to raise quality in early years settings is well documented (Munton, 2000; Nutbrown, 1998, Sylva, 2000) but such opportunities for further training and education also facilitate growth, security, belonging, esteem and self actualisation in individual participants. (Maslow, 1970; Rodd, 1998). If the formulation of policy and training is based on the assumption that practitioners are a homogenous group and training favours one strong influential maintained sector above the needs of another, a 'two way sophistication gap' may emerge (Katz, 1995 p216). This is divisive and polarises sectors to create a power elite who organise the field in their own interests (Mills, 1956).

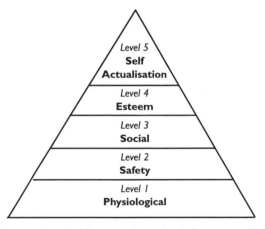

Figure 2 Hierarchy of Human Needs, (Maslow, 1970)

Maslow (1970) argues that it is difficult for an individual to progress through the hierarchy if their needs at the previous levels are not met (see figure 2). A strong determinant of progression is self-interest or motivation (Greenhalgh, 1994) and in the early years sector, training can be a motivational carrot. It reaffirms workers' value to the organisation, offering new career avenues and choices (McGivney, 1997; Pugh, 1996; Goleman, 1998). Figure 3 shows how Rodd (1998) has refined Maslow's hierarchy (1970) to use it as a tool to understand practitioners' motivation.

Maslow 1970	Rodd 1998
• Physiological needs	*Remuneration*
• Safety	*Employment security, structure, stability, law and order, protection and freedom from fear and anxiety.*
• Social	*To be part of a group, a social network, relationships with others*
• Esteem	*i. a need to demonstrate mastery and competence*
	ii. a need to feel appreciated and important and to gain a sense of respect from others
• Self actualisation	*Needs, personal growth and development, a desire to become the best they can be.*

Figure 3 Maslow, 1970 developed by Rodd, 1998 p50/1

Research design

The study comprises three small case studies of three preschool supervisors. Semi-structured interviews are the main source of data (Cohen *et al.*, 2000). Though case studies do not necessarily lead to generalised findings, it is appropriate to use a case study approach to further understand the experiences of practitioners in this under-researched field. What is really needed here is life-historical study, working over a one or two year timescale (Clough, 2000) to enable the stories of practitioners to be told and thus highlight the impact of policy changes within their situations, connecting the 'micro with the macro'.

Interviews

The women I invited to participate had all been supervisors for over five years with equivalent Preschool Learning Alliance training and qualifications. All were over forty and led at least five sessions per week in a rural voluntary managed group. All joined the EYDCP at the first opportunity, had consistently achieved good Ofsted inspections (Ofsted, 1999) but had attended few training courses during the past year. When approached, the supervisors were keen to participate and interested in my aim to give them a voice. All respondents were guaranteed anonymity, and offered the option to reflect upon our conversations and to raise concerns and add further thoughts or amendments if they desired (Cohen *et al.*, 2000).

I did not share my intention to liken them to Cinderella. I did not want them to feel I was inferring that they were inferior as practitioners. My intention was to highlight their particular needs within the voluntary sector and use their words to demonstrate the valuable contribution the voluntary sector makes to Early Childhood Education.

The interview schedule I constructed was in two parts. Firstly, I used short open-ended questions to establish their stories, and for the second part I utilised Rodd's (1998) adaptation of Maslow (1970) to design questions that would establish their physiological, safety, social, esteem and self-actualisation needs.

Interviews were tape recorded to ensure that I could return to the recordings to check nuances and allow me to observe all non-verbal responses during the interview without the distraction of making written records.

Some findings

All three supervisors have followed the same route into the profession, joining the groups as parents, and helping in sessions and then later participating in training offered locally by the PLA. This training had stimulated their interest to such a degree that they went on to become leaders of their groups, a traditional route to work in the voluntary sector (Crowe, 1973; McGivney, 1997).

One supervisor's story seems to encapsulate the many issues that currently face rural supervisors in the voluntary sector.

Ruth: Buttons Preschool

Ruth has been the group supervisor for six and a half years. Her involvement began nine years ago when she took her son to the toddler group attached to the preschool. She became involved with the management committee and served as group treasurer after enjoying participating in sessions as a parent helper. When her child left for school, she decided to embark on training with a view to working with children. She had worked as a cashier in a bank for eleven years, but hated the prospect of returning to banking and made enquiries with the Preschool Learning Alliance (PLA) to locate a suitable childcare course. She enrolled on a Diploma in Preschool Practice (DPP) course running locally. '*It was great. I met so many local preschool staff, we all worked together and I knew I had made the best decision for my future.*'

Halfway through the DPP course, she applied for the vacant position of preschool supervisor and has now run the group for six and a half years.

> *I mostly enjoy work now and at the time I began, it was so convenient fitting in the school times and as I don't drive I didn't have transport difficulties, as I work in the village where I live... I feel that it is very important that I am still available to support my child.*

She was positive about the changes that occurred since her involvement with the preschool.

> *I was a committee member when the Children's Act legislation (1989) was introduced and was actively involved in the changes necessary in the preschool.*

She found Ofsted inspections not so easy to deal with:

> *Ofsteds are a big stress! Our first experience was traumatic... The first inspector was very critical...the feedback was devastating and we were all in tears. We didn't have many action points but it was just her manner. The last two inspections have been great, we had no action points at all from the last one.*

One aspect of her role that has increased, though, is the paperwork and planning, especially since funding now includes some three year olds as well as all four years olds.

We have always maintained records but we now have to give more detail. The funding has created a pressure for places. We are now opening every morning and four afternoons to guarantee five sessions for every child. Although it is practically difficult – we are a small sixteen-place setting and it has been difficult to allocate places fairly and meet the needs of individual parents. Mornings have been most popular and I think that the children get the most out of the morning sessions. By the end of a busy day, they are tired and lethargic and quite honestly so are we (the staff). There are only the three of us and running a group is very demanding work. We try to recruit more staff but it's difficult in a village like this, people either have young children themselves or are working.

Ruth indicated that she felt more isolated now than in the early days. As a PLA member group, she had actively participated in the local branch activities:

There was a camaraderie between the preschool supervisors and the management committee representatives who went to branch meetings. I really enjoyed being part of something. We offered our thoughts on issues and these were fed back to County and National levels. We had a voice. But suddenly it all stopped. I haven't received any information about meetings for well over a year. If they are still running, they don't have very good publicity, we never hear anything.

Ruth reflected back to the good time and suggested that the downturn might have something to do with the loss of a very effective development worker who had supported the group.

I had a good relationship with her, she forged strong personal links with us and kept it (the branch) all going. After she left there was a long period when we had nothing. The new one (development worker) called, she was very nice, she visited us a year ago but we haven't seen her since. I think it is useful to receive support from the Centre and I appreciate that you provide a useful link with the Early Years Team. At this stage in my career I don't feel I need as much support as I used to. I tend to only give you a ring if I have a problem. I like the way I can tell you that we want a particular course and you can get it put on locally. Our staff with less experience would benefit from some inspiring workshops.

Support from the management committee is inconsistent from year to year and gradually the committee has diminished in number.

Going back ten years there was plenty of support. Now there is a core group of four people, it's so difficult to recruit people. Family life is so different now. There are more children wanting places, less helpers for parent rotas, a greater reliance on fewer people. When we had an accommodation crisis four years ago and it was vital that we moved from the village hall, everybody pulled together to ensure that we had some money behind us, we had an aim and we got there. Today there is no aim and the support has diminished, the new people have no idea of history and just accept the preschool as a community service. They don't understand that their contribution is vital – even when there isn't a crisis, we can't run without them.

Although Ruth obviously liked her work she did experience periods of pressure. Just recently she had tried to share the burden of paperwork with the other members of staff. None of them are paid for non-contact time so it was difficult to expect staff to work outside sessions.

I decided that if I motivated them (the staff) a little more they might become as enthusiastic as me. I was spending all my free time working for the group and thought, 'It's just me here, what is everybody else doing?' I introduced a staff appraisal scheme to motivate them. But that hasn't really lessened the burden because I feel so guilty when I have to keep asking them. The committee have let them both down at different times by refusing to pay for training, I am the only one with a full qualification so if I left there wouldn't be anybody trained to take my place. I do get lots of support from the village primary school both personally and for the group.

Asked about her physiological needs, Ruth made little reference to financial rewards.

Sometimes when I reflect on how much progress the children have made during the time they spend with us I feel very proud and that is reward enough. Although I am not dependent upon the money I earn (£6.00 per hour) I do see job advertisements for staff in other sectors and I feel that my contribution is under-valued. I think ' Hey! that's the same job I am doing'.

Asked what would make a difference, Ruth suggested that there would be less stress if there were more consistent management of the group:

Sometimes it's very much us – (the staff) and them (the committee) – the weak and the powerful – they have all the say.

She recounted a recent instance when the committee recruited a cleaner, advertising a higher pay rate than that of the preschool assistants. This had caused bad feeling and, as supervisor, Ruth had to deal with the discontentment and act as mediator.

Her response to questions about threats to her professional security was tinged with sadness:

Parents frighten me, they have a go behind my back to the committee over quite minor things, Can the preschool open two minutes earlier? Or can the children be given less to eat at snack time, because they are not eating their lunch? These are such minor things. I thought we were approachable, we organise the beginning and end of sessions so that parents can chat to key-workers – What is wrong with us? Why can't they come and talk with us?

Initially she had felt very vulnerable, but she did express gratitude for the support she received from parents who were trained teachers. After working together with them, she felt they were useful allies:

They understand what we go through. When teachers have taken leading positions on the committee they have been very helpful. They have a real understanding of what we are going through.

Information about local PLA branch meetings had not reached her and her attendance was restricted to specific venues because she didn't drive. A good relationship with the Foundation Stage teacher at the primary school was established. She felt that an opportunity to meet with other voluntary sector practitioners for mutual support would be useful.

Her responses to the questions about her self-esteem needs also highlighted the professional barriers she encountered with the maintained sector practitioners:

> *I haven't been on many of the courses recently. Some I have registered for were cancelled due to a lack of numbers. It's very difficult to get to the County town for others. I have attended a couple of networks. Some of the infant teachers seemed negative about changes to implement the Foundation Stage. There was only me and one other supervisor from the voluntary sector and we didn't have a lot in common with them (the teachers). The meeting was held at 3.45pm – this is still part of the teachers' working day. I have to attend in my own time.*

Ruth was unsure what she would be doing in five years time. She thought carefully before answering:

> *It's difficult to say what I will be doing in five years time. There are pressures in the group ... the relationship between staff and the committee. My son will move schools shortly – this is affecting my emotional state, my priorities are changing, I have new options. I have recently found out about Open University courses, they seem very interesting. I don't think that I could be an early years trainer.*

Conclusions

Ruth's story is similar to those of the other two women preschool supervisors in the study. So what can we learn from them?

My study suggests that the respondents looked *inwards* to the preschool fulfil their needs as early childhood practitioners. They do not recognise that professional development opportunities on offer could meet their practical and developmental needs. Their safety needs are not being met and they are insufficiently motivated to address their social needs (Maslow, 1970). They rarely meet with other voluntary practitioners and have few opportunities to reflect upon and debate early childhood educational practice. They feel threatened by and detached from other sectors and having had bad experiences, they have no wish to repeat them. By not addressing their own professional needs, preschool supervisors displayed little intrinsic motivations to further develop their own careers.

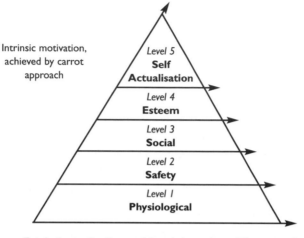

Intrinsic motivation, achieved by carrot approach

Level 5
Self Actualisation

Level 4
Esteem

Level 3
Social

Level 2
Safety

Level 1
Physiological

Extrinsic motivations achieved through a stick approach

This small-scale study also suggests a '*two-way sophistication gap*' between the supervisors and those who develop and implement policy (Katz, 1995). This is evident in the timing and location of training courses. It is also disappointing that the supervisors' responses suggest that they are at the end of their learning journeys rather than the beginning. A culture of lifelong learning has failed to reach them.

Preschool playgroup supervisors are employees within (often) poor management structures. However well-meaning the people who create and operate those structures might be, lack of continuity and insufficient underpinning of the knowledge required to deliver the Foundation Stage is a problem. The annual change of committee leads to short-term decision-making and uncertain staffing and practices. For example, a commitment to sustain the group in the short term by not committing funds to staff development increases pressures on those with qualifications to take the lion's share of responsibility. Consequently leaders are overworked and stressed and may be tempted to give up their supervisory role. This threatens the long-term sustainability of a preschool, particularly in rural areas where the pool of labour is small.

The preschool supervisors who participated in this study are not Cinderellas in their individual communities. Rather they are the invisible fairy godmothers within the early education sector, working for low pay in difficult and inconsistent management structures. Policy makers who create a multi-sector approach to Foundation Stage education must ensure that they do not become the wicked stepmothers by promising the voluntary sector preschool supervisors Maslow's self-actualisation without the means or support to access it. Now is the time to ensure that all voluntary sector practitioners are afforded a heartfelt invitation to the early education ball.

Recommendations for future research

This study offers an insight into the professional lives of voluntary sector supervisors in rural locations. It provides grounds on which to advocate support for such groups and has raised further questions for investigation. While the study was being conducted, a number of supervisors contacted me to tell me their stories; although these could not be included in the final study, their experiences in other counties mirror and affirm many of the issues raised within the study as reported here. Having established EYDCPs, it is surely timely for the UK government to conduct a review of the plight of voluntary sector practitioners and commit to a reform of the current remuneration and management structures (Webster, 2001).

To contribute to the knowledge and understanding of voluntary sector provision, a number of areas require further study:

- a comparative research project on a large scale, covering one county for example, interviewing voluntary private and maintained sector practitioners stratified through different geographical locations

- a longitudinal study charting the experiences of practitioners over a period of policy development

- a comparative study of rural, urban and inner city preschool supervisors to identify common characteristics of voluntary sector work and look at the additional benefits of social capital (Putnam, 2000)

- a case study of one voluntary sector preschool over one year that examines the perspectives of staff, committee members, parents and children.

References

Abbott, L. and Moylett, H. (1999) *Early Education Transformed* London: Falmer Press

Abbott, L. and Pugh, G. (1998) *Training to Work in the Early Years; developing a climbing frame*, Buckingham: Open University Press

Bourdieu, P. (1977) *Outline of Theory and Practice* Cambridge: Cambridge University Press

Brookfield, S. (1996) *Understanding and Facilitating Adult Learning* Buckingham: Open University Press.

Clough, P. (2000) *Understanding Teachers Lives; life historical research*, Module 4 Research Methods in Early Childhood Education, Dip/MA Early Childhood Education Sheffield: University Of Sheffield

Cohen, L., Manion, L. and Morrison, K. (2000) *Research Methods in Education* London: Routledge/Falmer

Crowe, B.,(1973) *The Playgroup Movement* London: George Allen and Unwin

DfEE (2000) *First Findings* Sudbury Suffolk: DfEE Publications

Edwards, R. Sieminski, S. and Zeldin, D. (1993) *Adult Learners, Education and Training* London: Routledge

Edwards, S.(2001) *Recognising the Value of Learning Through Play*, Oxford: The Oxford Times Education Yearbook 2001-2, The Oxford Times,

Gallagher, J. and Clifford, R. (2000) The Missing Support Infrastructure in Early Childhood, Vol.2 no.1 *Early Childhood Research and Practice,* http://ecrp.uniuc.edu/v2n1/ gallgher.html)

Goleman, D. (1996) *Emotional Intelligence* London: Bloomsbury

Goleman, D. (1998) *Working with Emotional Intelligence* London: Bloomsbury

Greenhalgh, P. (1994) *Emotional Growth and Learning* London: Routledge

Katz, L. (1995) *Talks with Teachers of Young Children* New Jersey: Ablex

Leadbeater, M. (1999) *To our Mutual Advantage* Speech delivered at the PLA From Play-dough to Plato Conference, 12th May 1999, Mermaid Theatre London

Maslow, A. (1970) *Motivation and Personality* New York: Harper and Row

McGivney, V. (1993) *The Learning Outcomes for Adults using Pre-school Groups* Leicester: NIACE

Mill, J.S., (1991) *On Liberty and Other Essays* Oxford: Oxford University Press

Mills, C.W. (1956) *The Power Elite* New York: Oxford University Press

Munton, T. (2000) The Iron Triangle *Nursery World* 17th February 2000

Nutbrown, C. (1996) *Respectful Educators, Capable Learners: Children's Rights in Early Education* London: Paul Chapman Publishing

Nutbrown, C. (1998) *The Lore and Language of Early Education* Sheffield: University of Sheffield

Ofsted (1999) *The Quality of Nursery Education, Developments since 1997-98 in the Private, Voluntary and Independent Sector* London: Ofsted Publications

Pugh, G. (ed) (1996) *Contemporary Issues in the Early Years* London: Paul Chapman Publishing

Putnam, R. (2000) *Bowling Alone* New York: Simon and Schuster

Robert, C. (2000) Distant Places, Diverse Spaces: early childhood professional development in isolated locations *Contemporary Issues in Early Childhood Education*, Vol 1, No 3, p277-286

Rodd, J. (1998) *Leadership in Early Childhood Education* Buckingham: Open University Press

Sylva, K. (2000) *The Effective Provision of Pre-school Education; A longitudinal study funded by the DfEE*, EPPE Symposium 7th to 9th September, Cardiff, UK.

Webster, S.D. (2001) Cinderellas in Lonely Castles: The perceptions of rurally located voluntary preschool supervisors, unpublished Masters Dissertation Sheffield: University of Sheffield

Williams, J. (2000) *Think Country Child* London: NCVCCO

Endword: researching the future

Cathy Nutbrown

Reflection

The accounts of small-scale research studies in this collection demonstrate the comprehensive nature of Early Childhood Education and the various ways in which it has changed and is changing. Early Childhood Education is different now: it is not shielded from the harsh political realities of society in the post-modern era, and the children it serves are learning to live in a world which is ever changing and continually vulnerable.

This book began with a reflection on the inevitability of change, and the chapters throughout have demonstrated how ownership of change through the active interpretation of policy can both empower professionals and challenge policy makers. For example, the first three chapters by Sue Allingham, Di Chilvers and Julie Bravery demonstrate the importance of understanding, critiquing and inter-preting assessment policies in the context of state provision for four year olds. They show how informed practitioners are positioned not only to understand but also to 'make' policy, as they transform requirements in to the lived experiences of teaching and learning. Debbie Critchley, in chapter 5, demonstrates what is possible when assessment is extended to the children and demonstrates their strategies for evaluating their own learning. Taken together, these opening chapters are an example of movement from policy, through critique, into the realities of daily practices for educators and ex-periences for children.

Early Childhood Education is changing, and it is healthy to see that discussions of curriculum are no longer confined to implementation of strategies for improving literacy and numeracy. Polly Dyer's work on emotional intelligence shows the importance of nurturing the makings of a civil society in the nursery classroom. Such work requires a considerable degree of risk on the part of educators, and depends on well grounded philosophical and moral principles which in turn are realised through a thoughtful pedagogy of understanding and interaction. It requires, too, an openness with parents in order to create a consistency of understanding as well as approach.

So, whilst the first part of the book begins with discussion of assessment and the difficulties imposed by targets, it concludes with two accounts by Christine Parker and Anne Kirkpatrick of work with parents which offer insight into the development of shared understandings of children's learning. These examples offer us a glimpse into the nature of teaching, learning and assessment in the Foundation Stage as seen through the eyes of practitioners, and they indicate the primary concerns of those working in the field.

The themes of social justice and the development of citizenship are strongly indicated in the second part of the book, which focuses on issues which any society must confront and consider if it is to develop a way of being which is inclusive of its members. Vicky Grant and Nicky Walters have examined aspects of gender and the impact of understandings of gender on the expectations of and for children and of the types of toys parents choose to buy for their children. They both concluded that practitioners need to be fully aware of the subtleties of gender difference and of stereotype, as they create curriculum and open up opportunities for young children.

The theme of *difference and diversity* is further developed in Gill Farmer's account of the use of persona dolls with students training for child care and education professions. The challenges faced by students as they identified and tried to address their own prejudices offer powerful lessons to all early childhood educators about the need to understand ourselves in order to understand others, in the cause of developing not just a tolerant but an inclusive society.

We can only speculate about the needs for professional development and personal reflection on the part of the education professionals involved in *Simon's Story*. In telling this story, Tracey Berry opens up an honest account of the experience of one child and one family to ask '*Does inclusion work*'? Perhaps we should ask 'Can we afford to let it fail?', for the consequences of a failure to include all citizens – whatever their age – are the perpetuation of an unjust and unequal community and a denial of the rights of citizenship for the more vulnerable.

Read against Polly Dyer's chapter, the work developed by Ramona Khan in Trinidad and Tobago provides a sharp reminder of the importance of treating children with civility and compassion, and of the need to question practice and develop services and practices in the context of the UN Convention on the Rights of the Child. The messages in Khan's chapter are important to heed; they are not the sole territory of two Caribbean islands. Positive strategies for helping children to live together amicably, without using physical punishment are issues for us all.

The final chapter in this collection gives an account of the experiences of some isolated Early Childhood Educators who are developing their work in the contexts of massive policy shifts which have brought an increase in expectation and accountability. Suc Webster demonstrates the importance of support and recognition for the service providers who have only recently been brought into the main-frame of early childhood provision.

Messages for the future

So what does this book tell us about future research in Early Childhood Education? First, it carries many messages about key themes for future research: whatever issues of curriculum and pedagogy are studied, they need to be researched in the context of educational communities and of society as a whole.

Second, it makes a statement about those who carry out research: early childhood educators who develop a research-informed stance to their practice and to the interpretation of policy have an important part to play in the development of future research in Early Childhood Education.

Finally, the contributions here demonstrate how reflective practitioners can develop their own enquiries by working together as a supported and supportive networked learning community, drawing on published research, developing appropriate methodologies and sharing their outcomes.

Researching the future in Early Childhood Education offers much and, as the contributors to this book have demonstrated, the combination of schools and other early childhood settings and services working with a University in order to develop their own research means that the sum of the whole is worth much more than each of those individual parts. The contributions in this book provide in-roads into the many territories still to be explored and offer strategies for positive policy development. The many issues raised set an agenda for practice and research in the future.

Author index

Subject index